"Bless those who persecute you;
bless and do not curse."

—Romans 12:14 (NIV)

WHISTLE STOP Café MYSTERIES

WHEN YOU WISH UPON A STAR

BECKY MELBY

Published by Guideposts
100 Reserve Road, Suite E200
Danbury, CT 06810
Guideposts.org

Cover and interior design by Müllerhaus
Cover illustration by Greg Copeland at Illustration Online LLC.
Typeset by Aptara, Inc.

ISBN 978-1-961126-82-4 (hardcover)
ISBN 978-1-961126-83-1 (epub)

Printed and bound in the United States of America
10 9 8 7 6 5 4 3 2 1

WHEN YOU WISH UPON A STAR

"Summer!"

Roxanne Britton practically squealed the word to her best friend, Caroline Davis. They had just stopped in front of Roxy's house, waving goodbye to Minnie Franklin, who continued to walk home.

"Shorts," Caroline agreed, clutching a handful of her plaid skirt. "Can't wait to be done with slips and dresses."

After tugging her damp blouse away from her skin, Roxy pulled a key from her purse. "I'm going to get the mail and grab some cooler clothes."

"Okay. Mom said she'd have a special treat for the last day of school, so hurry."

"I'll be there in a jiffy." She trotted up the sidewalk then paused and called back, "Hey. We're officially juniors."

"Upperclasswomen." Caroline held out her stack of class notebooks. "If it wasn't so hot, I'd say we should make a bonfire with these."

"Sounds like a good idea for a Friday night party at the camp."

Her suggestion was met with an arch of a perfectly shaped brow. "Wouldn't that be a gas? Let's talk to the gang and see if we can pull it off."

"It's going to be a clear night. We could work on our Star Finder badges."

"Great idea. Go change. We plan better in bare feet."

"Agreed." Roxy bounded up the steps to her front porch. The black metal mailbox squeaked as she opened it. Inside, she found two bills, a week-old copy of the Hollywood Citizen-News, the newest LIFE magazine, and a letter from Jade.

She glanced at the return address. Jade Tanaka, still at the same address, the adobe house near Wilton and Monroe in Los Angeles.

Not a detention camp.

She breathed a sigh of relief but then noticed with surprise that the letter was addressed to Mrs. Eric Britton. Not to Roxy but to her mother. That was strange.

Folding the mail with the letter on top, she tucked it under one arm and unlocked the front door. As she kicked off her loafers, the silence in the stuffy, dark

2

interior caused a hitch in her breathing, the way it always did.

Eight weeks ago—before her mother had been asked to serve a three-month stint at Walter Reed General Hospital in Washington, DC, with the US Army Nurse Corps—there would have been music playing on the phonograph when Roxy walked in from school. Her mother would have been singing "Tumbling Tumbleweeds" or "Empty Saddles" along with Bing Crosby while cleaning, baking, or painting another water-color landscape.

Six months ago, her father would have been at his drafting table in the room to her right, the one with the beveled glass door, designing homes for clients throughout east central Ohio. Not on a ship some-where in the Pacific.

But six months ago, the country had not been at war.

Staying with Caroline, her next-door neighbor and best friend since fifth grade, had sounded exciting when her mother and Caroline's had first proposed the idea of Roxy and her little sister, Diana, moving in with the Davises. But three months was feeling much, much longer than she'd anticipated.

Caroline's mother, one of the kindest women she knew, had been her second mom for years, but she'd never been fond of Mr. Davis, whose arbitrary rules were unreasonable and controlling. And the man was as narrow-minded as a person could be. She tried not to judge him too harshly. Caroline's brother, Steven, was stationed in France. That was Mr. Davis's reason for distrusting anyone with a German-sounding name. But Roxy's father was somewhere in the Pacific, fighting the Japanese, and that didn't make Roxy prejudiced against Japanese people.

Still—as she reminded herself every morning when he demanded the girls finish every bite on their breakfast plates—cooperating with his rules so that her parents needn't worry while they served was one small part she could play in the war effort.

Upstairs in her room, Roxy opened her bottom dresser drawer and pulled out the two pairs of shorts she owned. From the closet, she grabbed a short sailor jumpsuit, two lightweight dresses, and a couple of sleeveless blouses. "Bring on summer," she said out loud. Her words echoed strangely in the empty house.

She slipped out of her A-line skirt, full slip, and plaid blouse. She'd heeded the call for nylon stockings that could be used for making ropes and parachutes, resigning herself to wearing socks instead. She had kept a single pair of nylons tucked away for special occasions.

After putting on a shirt with navy and white stripes and a pair of baby-blue cotton shorts that belted at the waist, she perched on the bed and slid a letter opener under the flap of the letter from Jade.

Dear Aunt Luanne,

In your Christmas letter, you said we were all welcome to come and stay with you if the need arose. Well, Mother and Father have been forced to move. I intended to go with them, but Father was so heartbroken at the thought of abandoning his work that I have decided to defy the order and continue his translations.

I am leaving tonight and praying with every mile that I can get to you. I apologize for this short notice. I have tried calling you several times but haven't caught you at home. If it won't work for me to stay with you for any reason at all, I understand. I would never want to put you and your family in a danger-ous situation.

By the time you read this, I will be on my way. Again, please know I will understand if this doesn't work.

I pray for you, Roxy, Diana, and Uncle Eric daily. It will be wonderful to put my arms around you and catch up, even if it's for a short visit. I look forward to joining you for the Sunday church service you've told us about.

All my love,

Jade

The letter had been postmarked three days before. Jade could drive. Had she taken the family car? Or would she be arriving by train?

Roxy's heart began to pound in her chest. Jade was like a sister. They'd been raised together until five years ago. She would never turn Jade away. Could her dear friend stay here in the unoccupied house, hiding like a fugitive?

One thing was certain. She would not be welcome in Mr. Davis's home. Roxy would have to come up with something else. And for Jade, she would.

CHAPTER ONE

The August air was already thick and muggy on Friday morning when Debbie Albright arrived at the Whistle Stop Café, which she and her best friend, Janet Shaw, had owned for more than a year. As she walked through the door, she was startled to see Janet behind the counter, hands on her hips in a stance that reminded Debbie of an agitated referee.

"What's wrong?" Debbie gaped at her friend. In more than thirty years of friendship, she'd rarely seen Janet so visibly angry.

"This." Janet pushed her phone across the counter.

On the screen was their first one-star review. Her heart sank. They'd always received enthusiastic comments about their food and service. This one was from a tourist visiting Dennison for the first time.

> *The food and friendliness in this nostalgic café housed in a historic Ohio train depot lives up to the town's claim to be 'a great place to call home.' Even if you, like my wife and I, are only passing through, you'll walk away feeling like you've spent an hour with family.*

"Read it." Janet swatted at a bit of flour on the front of her T-shirt featuring the words LET'S DOUGH THIS! printed under a picture of a rolling pin.

Debbie held the phone closer and read the acerbic words out loud. "'Never have I received such poor service. I must have sat for half an hour waiting for someone to take my order and then another half an hour to receive my food. With all the hype I've read about this place, I expected something more than what you can get at any Midwest greasy spoon.'" Debbie felt her anger building as she read the final sentence. "'The depot museum was worth a drive, but don't waste your time at the café.'" She glanced up, knowing her expression likely mirrored Janet's. "'Greasy spoon'? And no one has *ever* had to wait half an hour to have their order taken."

"I know that, you know that, and our regulars know that. But what will this say to people who've never been here and find us online?"

"Who wrote this?" Debbie squinted at the small letters. "Gastro Gnome?" She inhaled sharply. "That lady—I think it was Tuesday. She wore a shirt that said 'Gastro Gnome.'"

"Now that you say that, I remember commenting on the cute gnome on her shirt," Janet said. "Pretty sure she didn't smile once, and I know she didn't tip."

"She told me she'd recently moved here with her son and his family. I got the impression she wasn't happy about the move."

"She lives here?" Janet grimaced. A timer went off behind her. "Time to fry doughnuts. We can't let this derail us."

Debbie rolled her eyes. "Save your railroad jokes for the customers. Ah, like this one."

Harry Franklin—followed closely by his black-and-white canine sidekick, Crosby—shuffled to his usual seat in front of the window then mopped his brow with a handkerchief. "In this heat, you can shut off your fryer and cook directly on the rails. Back in the day, I saw plenty of people down on their luck doing that."

Debbie smiled at the ninety-six-year-old, still handsome African-American who had come to the depot every morning for more than eighty years. Starting out as a porter in his teens, he'd gone on to be a conductor after World War II. Now, thirty years after retiring, he still came daily to eat breakfast and watch the trains. He would be a good one to sic on Gastro Gnome and set her straight.

Debbie pressed her lips together, holding back a laugh. "Makes a person count their blessings, doesn't it?" She set a glass of ice water in front of him. "Can I talk you into an iced coffee this morning?"

Harry's lined face scrunched. "I usually wouldn't say you can call it coffee once you pour it over ice, but I'm going to make an exception this morning. Patricia, crazy girl that she is, will want hers hot. What's in the bakery case today?" His granddaughter, local attorney Patricia Franklin, often joined him for breakfast.

"Janet made some puff pastry tarts filled with cream cheese and fresh fruit. Cool and light."

"We'll take two. I mean three." Harry winked. "Don't tell Patricia about the third one."

The bell above the door jingled, and Harry's granddaughter came in, chatting with another frequent customer. Ashling Kelly's long auburn hair was braided and coiled around her head like a crown. She wore a bright red T-shirt that said JILL OF ALL TRADES and walked with a slight limp most people wouldn't even notice, all that remained from a car accident nearly a year before. She waved at Debbie and took a seat at the counter.

"Morning, Ashling." Debbie stepped around the end of the counter and filled two glasses with ice. "The usual?"

"Yes, please. And when you and Janet have a minute, I want to ask you something."

After serving Harry and Patricia, Debbie set a chocolate-frosted doughnut and an iced coffee, heavy on the cream and sugar, in front of Ashling. She poked her head into the kitchen and called to Janet, who finished assembling an ice cream sandwich with giant chocolate chip cookies and popped it into the freezer on her way to the front. It was National Ice Cream Sandwich Day, and they were prepared to help the lunch crowd celebrate.

Ashling took a slurp of her drink then pulled a stack of brightly colored flyers from a canvas bag. "Would you mind posting a couple of these?"

Debbie examined the papers. Below an image of a magnifying glass were the words, *Looking for girls in grades 9–12 who want to make friends and make a difference!* The remainder of the text announced an informational Girl Scout meeting to be held in the high school cafeteria on August 7.

The last line on the page brought a smile to Debbie's face.

Questions? Contact Ashling Kelly, leader.

Janet's expression reflected the delight Debbie felt. Her daughter, Tiffany, had always been close with Ashling. "When did you become a leader?"

"Yesterday." Ashling practically vibrated with enthusiasm. "I mean, it was official yesterday. I enrolled in an online training class last month. I'm taking over for the current leader, who's due to have a baby any day."

"That's wonderful," Debbie said. "Is it a big job?"

"Yes and no. There are only five girls in the troop now, and I'm hoping to grow it. That's where the work will come in. I'm fully aware that some parents might not feel confident with such a young leader, so I'm turning to the seasoned, experienced, wise, confident women who have guided my life's journey. I beg them to come alongside me and impart wisdom to young, impressionable girls." As if the over-the-top words were not enough, she accompanied them with puppy-dog eyes and hands pressed together in a comically pleading gesture.

Janet laughed. "Has anyone ever said no to you?"

Ashling rested one fingertip on her chin. "Not that I can recall."

Debbie rolled her eyes. "How are we supposed to refuse after that?"

"You're not." Ashling lifted her cup and took a sip, her rosy, freckled cheeks plumping as she smiled around her straw. "Seriously, you two were the first people I thought of. You've both been such amazing encouragers this past year. I want to be that for girls who don't already have cheerleaders in their lives."

Debbie was surprised by the unexpected tightening of her throat. It had been a challenging year for Ashling. Eight months before, she'd been in an accident that had left her with a concussion and a broken leg, plus totaled the pickup truck she used for her business, Jill of All Trades. To look at her now, with the sun-kissed glow on her face, it was hard to believe she'd been in an induced coma in December, her skin almost as white as the sheets she lay on.

"How can we help?" Janet asked.

"Grandma has such cool stories of scouting when she was a girl. I want to teach the girls some old-school skills."

"I see why you came to us." Debbie made her voice wobble like someone twice her age. "You want someone who remembers life in the Dark Ages, before every kid had a cell phone and laptop. Well, you came to the right people. We were Girl Scouts in the old days when kids played outside, riding bikes and roller skating. We had one computer in the house, and it was dial-up." She gasped in mock horror.

"And if we wanted to watch a movie, we had to go the store and rent a VHS tape." Janet sighed and pressed the back of her hand to her forehead. "You have no idea how rough we old folks had it."

Ashling laughed. "I didn't mean—well, yes, I guess that's exactly what I meant. Minus the 'old' part. I want to draw on the experiences of people of *all* ages, especially former scouts. Like Girl Scouting through the ages."

Janet rested her fingertips on Ashling's hand. "Love it. You know we'll do anything we can to help you. I'd be happy to teach some baking skills."

Debbie chewed on her bottom lip. From the time she'd graduated college until less than two years before, her life had been consumed with a demanding corporate job in Cleveland and hanging out with friends in her limited free time. Besides reading and journaling, she'd never taken the time to develop any other hobbies.

Unless compiling stories of Dennison's Greatest Generation residents counted. "I could talk to the girls about journaling and preserving family histories."

Ashling beamed. "That would be wonderful. Thank you both. I knew I could count on you." She glanced at her watch then pointed to her untouched doughnut. "Can I take this to go? I've been talking and forgetting to eat. I have to be at a job in ten minutes, but I'll be back tomorrow. I'm grateful for any ideas you can come up with."

After Ashling left, Debbie turned to Janet. "Earlier this year, Kim had a Girl Scout display over in the museum. It was all about the scouts who volunteered during the war. Bet there'd be some interesting things in that collection if she still has it. I think it would help prospective scouts feel connected to the organization."

"That's right. She had a bunch of photographs and a couple of uniforms from the forties."

"And a handbook. It was displayed in the glass case. It's probably full of exactly the kind of nostalgic stuff Ashling wants to explain the organization through the ages." Debbie swept the café with her gaze. It wasn't a busy morning, but she wasn't sure she could bring herself to abandon Janet in case there was a rush.

"Go ask her." Janet laughed. "You'll be useless here until you find out if she still has it."

Debbie nudged her best friend with her shoulder. "Thanks. I'll be back in a jiffy."

"It's in a white library box. I know I labeled it. It's around here somewhere." Kim Smith, curator of the Dennison Depot Museum, brushed dark, feathery bangs away from her face as she scanned the contents of the small storeroom.

The room was not air-conditioned, and even after a couple minutes of searching, Debbie started to feel claustrophobic. She scanned shelves marked with labels like VINTAGE CHRISTMAS,

SALVATION ARMY BROCHURES, and LETTERS FROM HOME. Then she spotted it on a top shelf, a white box marked GIRL SCOUTS WWII. "Found it." She pulled a step stool close then climbed up, slid the box out, and handed it down to Kim.

"Good work. Let's get out of this oven," Kim said. "Take the whole box. I won't need it for a while, so I'm glad it'll be put to good use in the meantime."

Back in the café, Janet passed Debbie with two plates of bacon, eggs, and hash browns balanced on her forearm and a coffeepot in her free hand. Debbie set the box on the counter and lifted the lid. "I'm going to make sure the book is in here. That's all. Then I'm back to work."

"Sure you are. Don't worry about me. I can do it. All by myself."

Ignoring Janet's exaggerated sigh, Debbie examined the box's contents. Plastic zipper bags contained uniforms beside a stack of notebooks. When she lifted one, she saw the green spine of a cloth-covered book. It was the handbook she'd been hunting for.

"Hey, I've got a bit of history for you."

Debbie smiled as Harry approached, arm in arm with his stylish granddaughter. She'd heard many of his stories dozens of times, but once in a while a new one popped up. "What's that, Harry?"

He indicated the box. "My cousin Minnie was the first African American Girl Scout in Dennison. Must have been 1940 or so when she joined up."

Debbie had a vague recollection of meeting Minnie somewhere years ago. She rested a hand on Harry's forearm. "Ashling would love to hear that. She became a scout leader yesterday."

"Tell her I'm willing to pass on any questions. Minnie is always happy to share her wisdom." Harry saluted her with his to-go cup and walked toward the door with Patricia, Crosby at his heels. The group paused to talk to the next person walking through the door.

Debbie opened the front cover of the green handbook.

Happy 15th Birthday, Roxanne!
Hope the next few years of Girl Scouting are wonderful. We are so
proud of the kind and generous young woman you are becoming.
Love you so much, Mom and Dad
September 3, 1941

Across from the copyright page, which showed that the book had been printed in April of 1941, was a page with blanks filled in with dark blue ink.

THIS IS MY BOOK.
DATE: September 3, 1941
TROOP: No. 52
NAME: Roxanne Britton
ADDRESS: 626 Grant St., Dennison, Ohio

As she turned another page, something fell out and drifted to the floor by the door. A pressed flower. She bent to pick it up.

"Don't!" Harry's black leather shoe blocked her way. "Don't touch that, Debbie. It's monkshood. Also known as wolfsbane or aconite. It's deadly. Just touching it could kill you."

CHAPTER TWO

"H arry's right."

As Janet flipped over the Closed sign on the café door, Debbie set down her phone, which she'd used to research the dried flower on a paper plate in front of her. The brittle petals still held a tinge of purple. She'd used a plastic fork to lift it onto the plate then hidden it in an unused bottom cupboard until the end of the day. "It's highly poisonous, even by touching it. Your skin can absorb the toxins. I can't tell if it's still that dangerous in its dried state, but I don't think we should take any chances. It's called monkshood because it's shaped like the cowls worn by monks."

Janet slid onto the chair across from her, and Debbie showed her a photo of the deceptively beautiful purple blossoms. "They're pretty. I bet whoever pressed it in the book didn't know it was dangerous."

Debbie's phone vibrated, and a text message appeared on the screen. She smiled at the name. She'd been dating Greg Connor for several months now, and she was still in awe at this chance for the kind of happiness she'd almost given up on.

Have you seen this? Who is Gastro Gnome?

Greg, who was president of the Dennison Chamber of Commerce, had sent a screenshot of another scathing review, this one on the chamber's social media page. Similar words, but this one ended with, *You'd get better food at Floyd's Gas Depot.*

"Yikes," Janet said when Debbie told her. "What are we going to do about these?"

"Nothing." Debbie typed a quick response.

SAW IT. NOTHING WE CAN DO BUT TURN THE OTHER CHEEK AND HOPE OUR REGULARS COME TO OUR DEFENSE.

She showed her answer to Janet, who nodded. "Exactly right. We'll get through this."

"Yes we will." Debbie sent the text.

Janet picked up the thick green book. "I wonder which pages she pressed it between. Maybe that will tell us something." As she opened the book, something clear and yellow fell out.

Debbie grabbed it. "Cellophane." The material was dotted with tiny flecks of brown, faded green, and purple. Debbie dropped it onto the plate beside the plant. "If she kept the flower in this, it's very possible she knew it was deadly."

"She might have collected it for a plant identification badge. Maybe there were extra points for poisonous plants. I'd be on board with that, as long as the girls were taught how to handle them safely."

"You would have made a great scout leader." Debbie tapped the paper plate. "Have you ever seen these growing around here?"

"No, but I'm no expert."

Debbie typed in *wild monkshood Ohio* and read the top result to Janet. "There's one kind called Northern wild monkshood. It's on the federal threatened species list, and our state's endangered species list. This says it's found in three disjunct places—"

"Disjunct?"

Debbie checked the definition in a new tab. "It means they're not continuous. In this case, I'd say it refers to three separate regions that aren't right next to each other. Okay, moving on. Northern wild monkshood is found in southwest Wisconsin and northeast Iowa, the Catskills, and northeast Ohio. Apparently it prefers shady spots, cool places near streams, and on cliffs and 'algific talus' slopes."

"Algific talus?" Janet echoed.

Again, Debbie searched for a definition. "They're hillsides made up of broken rocks with vents connecting to ice caves that keep a stable temperature year-round." She swiped to another page. "There's a map. Monkshood grows in a couple nearby counties but not here."

"Now."

Debbie tipped her head to one side and stared at her friend. "Huh?"

"That's where it's growing now. What about eighty years ago?"

"Good point." Debbie found another article about monkshood, then felt a sudden chill that did not come from the air conditioner. "Monkshood is also known as aconitum. Other names for it are leopard's bane, wolfsbane, Devil's helmet, blue rocket, and Jupiter's Helm."

Janet leaned forward, eyes wide. "Wasn't that hill called Jupiter's Helm? The one above the cave at Camp Saundustee?"

"The really, really cold cave with the stream running through it." Debbie nodded. "The one we called Ice Cave at the Girl Scout camp."

Barefoot, in shorts and an old, worn tank top she'd never leave the house in, Debbie settled on her couch and thanked God for the invention of air-conditioning. She ran her index finger along a beaded glass of lemonade then held the glass to her forehead. The thermometer had hovered slightly below ninety all afternoon, so it wasn't as hot as some days. But combined with 90 percent humidity and working beside multiple machines that put off plenty of heat, she'd come home feeling drained.

The antidote for her exhaustion sat in front of her on the coffee table in a white cardboard box.

She lifted the lid, set it on the floor, and took out the Girl Scout handbook. Opening to the "This is My Book" page, she stared at the name and the address. *Roxanne Britton*. She didn't know any Brittons, but Roxanne had probably married. Was she still alive? Picking up her phone, she started with an obituary site she'd used before. She put in all the information she had, but got no results.

She tried a popular social media site next. Not that she thought a woman who was likely in her nineties by now would be active on social media, but she had a couple of friends who had started accounts for grandparents to keep them in touch with extended family. Twenty-seven Roxanne Brittons popped up, none of them born before 1960.

She moved on to the address. *626 Grant Street*. On her maps app, she found the street view. She recognized the house. After all, it was only a few blocks away.

Picking up the book again, she ran her finger across its edges. The pages fell open, and she stared at a ticket stub from State Theater on Main Street in Uhrichsville. The theater had been demolished at least a decade before she was born, but she knew where the building had stood. She flipped the ticket over. There were words on the back, tiny script in blue ink.

Mrs. Miniver - 6/26/42

C, M, & I disguised J & snuck her in!

Her phone dinged with a text message from Greg.

PLANS FOR TONIGHT? JAXON IS AT A PARTY, AND JULIAN BAILED ON OUR MOVIE NIGHT IN FAVOR OF VIDEO GAMES WITH FRIENDS. I'M CRAVING BUONA VITA'S EXCELLENT FOOD AND WOULD LOVE FOR YOU TO JOIN ME.

Greg was raising two boys on his own after losing his wife to cancer some years before. Jaxon would be starting his sophomore year of high school in a couple of weeks, and Julian would be in eighth grade.

She would never refuse an invitation to dinner with him. And as a history lover, he might find the book as interesting as she did.

With a spring in her step, she ran upstairs and took a quick shower, washing away the heat of the day and the smell of hard work. She dried her hair, used a flat iron to shape it so that it framed her face, and then added a light touch of makeup. In this heat, she'd likely "glow" it off in an hour. She smiled as her father's words drifted up from a long-ago memory. She'd come in from playing basketball with a neighbor boy and, echoing him, announced that she was "sweating like a pig." In mock horror, Dad had corrected her, "Ladies do not sweat, my dear. They glow."

Well, tonight she'd likely be glowing substantially, so a lightweight cotton sundress was in order. By the time Greg picked her up, she felt like a whole new woman.

His approving smile certainly didn't hurt. She returned the compliment. "I like that shirt. It brings out the blue in your eyes."

"Glad you approve." He opened the passenger door as they reached his car. "AC awaits, my lady." He got into the driver's seat and buckled his seat belt. "Pretty cool responses to Gastro Gnome's blog post, huh?"

"She has a blog?" A sick feeling settled in Debbie's stomach at the thought of even more vitriol spewed about her business online. "I only saw the review she put on our social media page and the one you sent me."

"Then you've gotten the gist of it. I got the scoop at the barbershop, where I hear all my local news. Apparently, she was a big-name food critic in New York City a while back and still has a huge following. She moved here with her son and his family a few weeks ago. Sounds like the café is her first victim since the move."

"A food *critic*?" Her voice squeaked. "This could be devastating."

"Not according to your customers. You should read what they're saying."

She took out her phone, found the Gastro Gnome blog, and started reading the comments out loud. "'The café is the best thing that ever happened to this town. I've never had to wait, and I've never been disappointed with the fabulous meals and bakery.' How sweet. 'Janet and Debbie are the most gracious, hospitable restaurant owners I've ever met. I've never had to wait too long, and they have the best doughnuts in the state.'" Around the fifteenth comment, she pressed her hand to her heart. "I haven't felt this loved in a long time. It's amazing to see our regular patrons going to bat for us."

Greg sent her a quick smile. "Everyone in this town loves the Whistle Stop, and you."

His tone sent a stampede of goose bumps up her arms. She grounded herself by taking the Girl Scout handbook out of her purse. She filled him in about Ashling's new role and finding the flower. She'd left the plant at home, in a zipper bag on a high shelf in her closet. Even the thought of someone accidentally touching it gave her the willies.

"I understand why a teenage girl would want to keep a corsage or a flower from a boyfriend, but why would someone save a poisonous flower?" Greg asked.

"She probably didn't know it was dangerous. Although Janet has a theory about poisonous plants being worth extra points."

Greg chuckled. "I hope she's wrong about that. But it does make sense that Roxanne might have collected it to earn a badge."

"Makes me wonder if she was affected by the toxins when she picked it."

When Greg parked at the restaurant, Debbie showed him the gaps between the top edges of some of the pages. "I found something else in here that raised some questions. That's your teaser for the rest of the evening. Anyway, there are other things tucked into it that might be marking pages. I was planning on spending the whole evening perusing the book, and I'd much rather do it with you."

"Nothing goes better with Italian food than a little monkshood and mystery."

"That's the spirit."

They got out of the car, and he took her hand as they walked toward the front door. To someone passing through town, the storefront resembled any little hole-in-the-wall restaurant, but once inside, the decor and rich aromas erased any notion of it being a nondescript eatery.

Once they were seated, Greg studied the menu. When Debbie didn't even reach for hers, he said, "I take it you aren't going to be adventurous tonight."

"I've tasted everything they have to offer, and I am a woman who knows her own mind. It doesn't get better than homemade spaghetti noodles. I spent more than twenty years eating out several times a week in Cleveland, and I never found spaghetti as good as they make here."

"Well, I like a woman who knows her own mind." He held her gaze long enough for her to be quite sure there was a dual meaning to his words. Though neither of them had said it yet, she wasn't hiding the fact that she knew her own mind about her feelings for him.

After they ordered and the server took their menus, Greg returned the conversation to the book. "Where did Kim get it?"

"I didn't think to ask. I'm going to do that right now." She fired off a quick text to the museum curator.

"What else did you find in there?"

She handed him the book, open to the movie ticket. "Read what's on the back of the ticket stub."

He did, then frowned. "Who are C and M, and why did they disguise J?"

"Exactly."

Greg put the ticket back, then flipped to another page holder. He pulled out a folded sheet of paper. "Wonder what this is. Love note? Secret message?"

She took the note and carefully opened the first fold and then the second, revealing the page. There were three groupings of small hand-drawn stars, black except for one red in each, connected by lines that had been drawn using a ruler or some kind of straight edge. Next to each grouping were two letters. One was labeled *HH*, the next *CC*, and the third *MB*. Across the top of the page, hand-written block letters spelled out *Star Finder Badge*. "It's a constellation map."

Greg leaned in. "Or that's what we're supposed to think it is."

Debbie shot him a questioning glance. "What do you mean?"

"Two years ago, the boys and I went to a weeklong astronomy camp in Michigan. On the last day they had a contest to see who could recognize the most constellations. There are eighty-eight known constellations. By the end of that week, we could each name more than half of them. Not that that makes me an expert or anything, but…" He took in the page once more. "I don't recognize any of these."

Roxy tried to appear calm and casual as she sauntered along the sidewalk on Friday morning. Just a girl with nothing on her mind on the first day of summer break. She tried to whistle, but it came out off-key, so she hummed the song that had come to her during the night when her racing thoughts wouldn't allow sleep. The words to "Walking the Floor Over You" didn't fit her current turmoil, but the sad lyrics had the benefit of slowing her steps as she walked to the depot.

Jade's letter was tucked in her back pocket. She needed to find out when Jade might arrive if she were coming by train, but she didn't know how to go about it. As she walked, she devised a plan. She'd say she and her mother were planning a trip to California, and she wondered how long it would take them to get there. If anyone asked, she could say they wanted to visit her aunt and uncle. They did want to visit the Tanakas. No one needed to know they were strictly her honorary aunt and uncle.

The problem was that she knew too many people who worked at the depot. Since the war began, she *and her mother—and most of her friends and their mothers—had volunteered at the canteen, serving sandwiches and cookies to the soldiers who arrived daily on troop trains. Everyone knew her mother was gone, and that she and Diana were staying with the Davises. Nothing about Jade's arrival, not a hint of it, could reach Mr. Davis.*

She rounded a corner and stopped. Across the street, Francie Reese, her Girl Scout leader, was out in her yard, kneeling by her garden. Her back was toward Roxy, so she could keep on walking and not be noticed. But didn't she need someone to confide in? If she could trust any adult, it would be Francie.

Still pondering, she kept walking. Francie was always starting discussions about doing the right thing. Roxy had told her about Jade, about the fear that she and her family would be sent to a camp. Francie had shown nothing but compassion. What would she say was the right thing to do if Roxy told her Jade was coming here? Would she help her find a place for Jade to stay? A secret hideaway where she could continue her father's work of translating Christian books into Japanese, where no one would find her and send her back to California...or to whatever state her parents had been sent to.

Or would Francie say the right thing was to contact the authorities and betray her friend's trust?

Since her father enlisted, Roxy had read the newspaper every night. Now that she was living with the Davises, she'd often get up after Mr. Davis had gone to bed to grab the paper and read it by the light of the small bedside lamp in the room she shared with Caroline. She didn't know for sure that he would have objected to her reading it, but she tried to make her moves in silence around him, never sure what would set him off.

She knew about Public Proclamation No. 4, which ordered the forced evacuation and detention of Japanese Americans living on the West Coast. The residents were sometimes given no more than forty-eight hours' notice. Refusing to comply could be punished by a year in prison and a $5,000 fine. Did that law apply to Jade, who was barely sixteen? Roxy didn't know, and she didn't know whom to ask.

Where were Aunt Miko and Uncle Ken? There were "relocation centers" in Arkansas, Wyoming, Arizona, and Utah. If Jade were caught, would she be reunited with her parents? Or would she be sent to prison?

When Roxy reached the depot, she waved at depot volunteer Eileen Turner as she walked out of the building, and then at Minnie's cousin, Harry Franklin. Harry was a year younger than she and Minnie, and he was always at the depot, watching the trains and talking about how he was going to get a job as a porter as soon as he was old enough. He knew more about trains than anyone she knew.

Did he know about the schedules too?

"Hey, Harry," she called to him. "I have a train question. How long would it take me to get to Los Angeles?"

Harry rubbed his chin. "Well, that'd be around twenty-five-hundred miles I think, so if the train was traveling at forty-five miles per hour and needs to stop for water every hundred miles but doesn't make any longer stops, my best guess, unless you had to change trains, which you probably would a couple of times, would be about sixty-two hours."

Roxy felt her eyes widen. "How did you figure that out so fast? You're a genius!"

The compliment seemed to embarrass him, but she caught the faintest smile before he ducked his head. "I hear there's a Girl Scout shindig out at Saundustee tonight."

"Yep. We're going stargazing."

"I've explored out there a few times. It's sad to see those half-built cabins. Think they'll finish the camp after the war?"

"I sure hope so. We've all looked forward to—" She froze, sure for a fraction of a breath she could hear angels singing. She reached out and clasped the arm of the boy in front of her. "Harry, I'll say it again. You really, truly are a genius."

As he stared back at her in bewilderment, she whirled on her heels and ran.

Cabins. *Hidden in the woods in a Girl Scout camp five miles east of town, partially developed before the war and abandoned when the funding had been cut before construction could resume that spring. Even with the funding, most of the construction workers were probably overseas or working for the war effort.*

Cabins. *Half-finished, yes. No windows, but they had sides and floors and roofs. Enough to keep out the elements and make a cozy little hideaway. Her thoughts spun. There were piles and piles of lumber at the camp. What would it take to make a bed and a table? Could three girls, working together, transform a half-finished cabin into a home overnight?*

CHAPTER THREE

*A*fter their server cleared their plates and took Greg's credit card, Debbie spread a napkin on the table then ran her thumb across the edges of the handbook in search of more treasures. The pages parted, and she removed a yellowed newspaper clipping.

Greg slid out of his side of the booth and came to sit beside her so they could both read it easily.

FOUR TONS OF SUGAR GONE MISSING

Eighty 100-pound bags of sugar disappeared from a rail-car at the Dennison, Ohio, train station in the early morning hours on May 31. The sugar, from Great Lakes Sugar Company in Paulding, Ohio, was picked up in Van Wert and was en route to Camp Ritchie in Cascade, Maryland. The Pennsylvania Railroad train had stopped for engine repair in Dennison. Sometime between midnight and 4 a.m., the merchandise car carrying the sugar was broken into and emptied. According to authorities, no witnesses have come forward and there are no suspects yet. With sugar prices now up by 18%, it is assumed it will be sold on the black market.

"Ever hear about this?" Debbie asked the history lover beside her.

Greg shook his head. "Sugar was probably one of the easiest things to sell on the black market once it was divided into smaller bags." He flipped the clipping over, revealing part of an ad for five-cent Pepsi-Cola. "Check it out. 'Made while you watch.'"

Debbie read the bit of copy that hadn't been cut off. "'Fine in flavor. Tops in taste. Big in size.'" She tapped the small print near the bottom. Big Ten-Ounce Glass! "Wonder what they'd call a two-liter bottle."

Greg studied the article again. "What year was this?"

"Sometime in the forties if it was stuck in there during the time Roxanne would have been in Girl Scouts." Picking up her phone, she typed in *black market Dennison Ohio WW2*. Nothing. She took out *Dennison Ohio*, but no helpful resources appeared. "We'd be better off asking Kim." She stuck the paper back between the pages then slid the book over to him. "Your turn to dig for treasure."

After a few more pages, they spotted a torn scrap of blue paper with a name and four numbers. *Francine Reese 2168*

"That could be a phone number. Know any Reeses?" she asked.

Greg's brow furrowed. "I went to grade school with a Stuart Reese. I think he went to a private high school. No idea where he is now."

"There's a building out at the Girl Scout camp called Reese Hall. Probably not a coincidence. I wonder who Francine is. Or was."

Greg gestured to Debbie's phone. "Everyone is findable these days, right?"

"Right." Debbie took in the crowd of people waiting for tables outside then checked the time and was shocked to realize they'd been there two hours. "Maybe we should continue this another time."

"Julian would love to see all this. He's gotten hooked on a series of historical mysteries recently. I can't promise he won't concoct some wild hypotheses about the monkshood, but that's more likely to be entertaining than anything else. Would you mind if I brought him over sometime this weekend?"

Him. Not them. She had a great rapport with Greg's younger son, but Jaxon still wasn't thrilled with her presence in their lives. "Why don't all of you come over for an early supper tomorrow? That way the boys will still be able to make plans with their friends afterward if they want to."

"You're sure?"

"Yes. Is four thirty too early?"

"Sounds perfect. In the meantime, I'll do some star research." He pulled out his phone and snapped a picture of the "constellations."

"And I'll talk to Kim at work tomorrow. We'll get to the bottom of this." When she picked up the book, an index card slid halfway out. Penciled words on the faded lines were barely discernable.

> *All parts of the* Aconitum *genus, also known as monkshood, are extremely poisonous. Severe poisoning can result from ingesting monkshood, but the poisons can also be absorbed through the skin. Symptoms can show up immediately or hours after contact and may include abdominal pain, nausea, vomiting, diarrhea, chest pain, shortness of breath, dizziness, irregular heartbeat, numbness, tingling, and weakness.*

There was a slight breeze on Saturday afternoon, making eighty degrees seem almost comfortable. Debbie set four plates on the little round table on the porch. It was still too hot for a heavy meal, so she'd arranged a tray with everything needed for do-it-yourself submarine sandwiches and chips. While pondering something light to serve for dessert, she remembered the two boxes of Girl Scout cookies she'd stashed in her freezer. They would do nicely.

She had a few minutes before Greg and either one or both boys arrived, so she sat on the porch and consciously let every muscle in her body relax. The cookies tempted, but she resisted, deciding instead to read the little blurbs on the packages, which led to questions about the first Girl Scout cookies. A quick search online brought some enlightening information.

In 1917, five years after Juliette Gordon Low started Girl Scouts in the United States, the first cookies were homemade by scouts and their moms. The Mistletoe Troop in Muskogee, Oklahoma, sold them in its high school cafeteria.

A few years later, the Girl Scout magazine, *The American Girl*, published a cookie recipe. Throughout the twenties, scouts across the country sold home-baked sugar cookies door-to-door for twenty-five to thirty-five cents a dozen.

In the late 1930s, the first commercially baked cookies were sold. During World War II, due to shortages of flour, sugar, and butter, Girl Scouts raised funds by selling calendars instead of cookies.

"Might as well give in to the temptation."

Greg's voice startled her, and she laughed as she raised her head, realizing the cookie boxes still sat on her lap.

Julian was right behind his dad. At first, she thought just the two of them had come, but the sound of slow footsteps on the porch steps told her Jaxon had tagged along too, whether willingly or reluctantly.

They took their seats. Hammer, the Connors' black-and-white border collie, found a shady spot on the cool concrete sidewalk. Debbie offered a blessing then invited her guests to dig in.

The sliced cheese and cold cuts disappeared in record time. Julian's eyes lit up when she opened the Thin Mints and Samoas. Jaxon, while keeping a cool exterior, didn't hesitate to dive into the boxes when they were passed around. Debbie and Greg savored a few while sipping iced tea and watching the boys consume their weight in chocolate, mint, caramel, and toasted coconut.

When Greg called a halt to the cookie consuming, the boys thanked her for the meal and cleared the plates without prompting from their father. Debbie didn't miss the gleam of pride in Greg's eyes.

"Who's up for some research?" Debbie asked.

"Me," Julian said eagerly.

"Not before you wash those hands, young man," Greg said. "You're not going to handle a historical artifact with chocolate all over your fingers."

Debbie stood to one side, watching the three of them playfully nudging each other out of the way and tossing a towel back and forth. She longed to jump in, but caution restrained her. She wouldn't win Jaxon's favor by inserting herself into every situation involving his family.

What would it be like to have that kind of camaraderie on a daily basis? Of course, it wasn't all fun and laughter. Even if—no, *when*— she was finally able to break through Jaxon's wall, it would take time to adjust to so much togetherness. She was used to having her own space and regulating the noise level in her home. Could she handle the occasional spat that was inevitable when sharing space with others, especially when some of them were growing into young adults?

That wasn't something to ponder at the moment. For now, she would merely enjoy the fun.

Julian hung the towel on its hook. "Dad showed us the drawings that look like constellations. We searched through every star chart in our books and online and couldn't find a match. I think Dad's right. They're supposed to make someone think they're constellations, but they're really a secret treasure map."

Debbie tapped Julian's shoulder with her fist. "That imagination is either going to serve you well someday or get you in big trouble." She took a notebook and pen from a kitchen drawer. "How about you be our secretary? You can record everything we find in the book, and then maybe we can come to some logical conclusions."

"Logic is boring." Julian took the notebook with a mock scowl.

Debbie led the way to the kitchen table where she had spread out their findings. The boys took seats, and she showed them the Girl Scout handbook and the inscription on the *This is My Book* page, then told them about finding the flower and what she'd learned from Harry and her online research.

"At first, I thought Roxanne, or whoever saved the flower, might not have known it was toxic. But that could have meant she was affected by picking it. When we found this"—she showed them the cellophane—"we wondered if she knew it was dangerous."

"And then we found this," Greg added, pushing the index card toward them.

"So, assuming she wrote this, she knew what she had," Julian said. "Which means she had a plan for it."

Jaxon gave a long-suffering sigh. "Right. And what would that plan be?"

Debbie intervened. "Probably to earn a Plant Finder badge."

"Nah." Julian's eyebrows shot up. "I bet she put monkshood in Girl Scout cookies and sold them to her victim. Or victims." He jumped to his feet and reached across the table for the paper labeled *Star Finder Badge*. Waving it in the air, he said, "The fake constellations mark all the places where Roxanne's victims lived. Or were buried."

Greg shrugged apologetically. "It's possible that raising them on a steady diet of mysteries has tainted their young minds."

"On the contrary, I'm sure it sharpened their senses," Debbie replied. "You should write down your theory, Julian."

"You seriously think a Girl Scout plotted murder by monkshood?" Jaxon directed the question at his brother, but Debbie had the feeling it was intended for her ears for encouraging Julian's wild imaginings. He picked up the article about the shipment of sugar. "The black market? That's like organized crime stuff. Right here in little ol' Dennison?"

Debbie nodded. "I'm waiting to see if Kim Smith knows anything about it."

Julian peered over Jaxon's shoulder. "Maybe the Girl Scouts ran out of sugar to make their cookies, so Roxanne poisoned the train engineer and stole the sugar. She's not the bad guy. She's actually a hero. If not for her, there might never have been another Girl Scout troop in America."

Debbie laughed. "You might be onto something." She told them what she'd read about the shortage of cookie ingredients during

World War II then slid the handbook across the table to Julian. "See what else you can find."

Julian riffled through the pages until the book fell open, revealing a small round object in the center. He leaned in. "It's a patch with a flower on it."

Jaxon tapped his finger on the lefthand page. "There's a picture of it. It's the Wild Plant Finder badge."

A sigh came from Greg's youngest. "That's really all this is about? She was trying to earn a dumb badge?"

"Sorry, boys. No murder or mayhem." Debbie smiled at Julian, who was grumbling under his breath.

"We still have a mystery, though." Greg picked up the movie ticket and showed the boys what was written on the other side.

The spark returned to Julian's eyes. "Who is 'J,' and why did they have to use a disguise to sneak him or her into a movie?"

Jaxon grabbed the book. "My turn." He flipped several pages, stopping when he came to a piece of card stock the size of a business card with an embossed border. On it were three symbols and three numbers that appeared to have been hand-drawn with black ink.

マタイ 5:44

The back of the card featured two lines in the same ink.

Roxy, this is our mission.

Jade

"Jade could be 'J,'" right?" Jaxon examined the back of the card again. "Is it a code?"

"It could be Japanese," Greg said.

"I know how to find out." Jaxon pulled his phone out of his pocket and took a picture of the card. "An exchange student from

Japan is staying with Mindy Porter's family. I met her once. Her name is Asuka." He typed a message. "And now we wait."

Julian reached for the notebook. "So, we have a dried deadly flower and some facts about it, a movie ticket with a note on the back about someone who may or may not be named Jade being disguised and snuck into the theater. Then there's something that resembles a constellation map, a Wild Plant Finder badge, a newspaper article about stolen sugar, a paper with the name Francine and some numbers on it, and weird symbols that might be Japanese and—wait a second." He sat up straight in his chair.

"What is it?" Debbie asked.

"What if we're wrong about Roxy? What if she wasn't just collecting the monkshood and the information about it to earn the badge? What if this"—he pointed at the numbers on the business card—"is a time of day? Maybe the Japanese symbols say something like 'Meet me' and then the numbers are for the time of day, 5:44. It's when they're going to complete their mission—the time Roxy and Jade were going to poison all the Girl Scout cookies going to the houses on the star map that isn't really a star map."

Debbie thought some of that sounded plausible, such as the meeting time message and that the star map might be a different kind of map. But for Roxy and Jade's sake, she hoped Julian was wrong about the rest of it. She didn't want to consider the idea that the two girls might have had sinister motives—and that she might have been unknowingly getting inside the head of a killer or two.

CHAPTER FOUR

*D*ebbie had planned to sleep until her alarm went off at eight on Sunday morning, but she woke a few minutes after six thirty, feeling hot and sticky despite the constant hum of the air conditioner. Today was predicted to hit ninety-seven. Though she preferred T-shirts and capri pants for most of the summer, this day required something light and airy.

She pulled a loose-fitting shift dress from its hanger. Large pink and purple flowers and green leaves splashed across the white, breathable fabric. Sleeveless and with a scoop neck, it could easily be dressed up or down. She grabbed a light cardigan, the same pink as the peonies on the dress, and a pair of white sandals. With a necklace and earrings of small pearls, it would be just right for church. Janet and her husband, Ian, had invited her for lunch, and she knew that by the time she helped Janet set the table, she'd be barefoot, bare-armed, and sans pearls.

At church, she sat behind Janet and Ian, their daughter, Tiffany, and Ashling. A shuffle of feet brought her attention to Greg and the boys sliding into the pew beside her. Greg leaned close to Debbie's ear. "Jaxon heard from the foreign exchange student."

"What do the characters mean?"

At that moment the first hymn began. Greg put his finger over his lips, his eyes dancing.

She scowled, then stood as the music swelled. In the next few moments, she let the words and music flow around and through her, forming a prayer in her heart. *I want to know You, Lord. I want to know Your voice and respond without hesitation. I want to hear You when You call, to always follow and never charge ahead of You. Lord, I want to love You more.*

Pastor Nick Winston was one of the most approachable, down-to-earth men she had ever met. His messages managed to combine a blend of deep scriptural truth with anecdotes and humor, a method that made his key points resonate and stick. Today, he focused on the need for listening to God when He whispered in that "still, small voice." Debbie's attention heightened when Pastor Nick said, "Sometimes those whispers, those little nudges from the Holy Spirit, don't make sense. Sometimes that's because the thing He wants us to pay attention to isn't for right now. It's to be tucked away for future use."

The words resounded in her spirit like divine confirmation. Maybe investigating the things they'd found in the Girl Scout book would prove to be nothing more than an interesting pastime. Or maybe it would lead her to something bigger, something God wanted her to learn or act on.

After the service and fellowship, she met Greg outside. She didn't bother with small talk. "What's the translation?"

"Just a heads-up, it's a bit anticlimactic."

"Another disappointment?"

"I'll let Jaxon tell you." He spotted Jaxon with a group of friends and called him over.

Jaxon left the group and joined them. She greeted him, careful not to make her voice overly cheery. "I hear the translation of the 'the mission' was a bit underwhelming."

"Yeah." He pulled out his phone. "This is from Asuka."

It's a Bible verse. Matthew 5:44, which says "But I tell you, love your enemies and pray for those who persecute you."

Of course, if this was written in the 1940s, it would probably have been in the King James Version. "But I say unto you, Love your enemies, bless them that curse you, do good to them that hate you, and pray for them which despitefully use you, and persecute you." Sorry, I'm a bit of a Bible nerd.

She had ended the text with a smiling emoji.

Julian joined them as Debbie handed the phone back to Jaxon, saying, "Unless there's some kind of hidden message, Roxy and Jade were probably not involved in a plot to serve up poison cookies."

"Yeah." Julian's shoulders slumped as he gave a long sigh.

Debbie gave him a sympathetic smile. "I'm still curious about why she kept that newspaper clipping. I'm waiting to hear something from Kim."

The boy perked up again. "Yeah. Maybe I'm still right, even if we can't see how."

Debbie closed her eyes for a moment, then gave Greg an apologetic grimace. "I'm sorry. I think I may have exacerbated what his mystery books started."

Debbie propped her bare feet on a chair on Ian and Janet's covered side porch. Ian had gone to help the neighbor across the road, whose car wouldn't start. Tiffany and Ashling were in the house cleaning up after lunch. They'd offered to make fajitas and handle cleanup so, in Ashling's words, "the not-old-but-extremely-wise women can put their feet up."

The not-old women hadn't argued.

Debbie appraised her best friend's face. "How are you handling the impending goodbye?" At the end of the month, Tiffany would return to college in Cleveland. Though it was still a few weeks away, Debbie recognized the signs that Janet was dreading the day.

"Trying not to be weepy and clingy for her sake." Janet took a sip of lemonade and offered her a tremulous, unconvincing smile. "We know people whose kids are heading to school in Miami and Seattle. One's heading to Paris and won't be home until Christmas break. This shouldn't be such a big deal."

"Says who? Your feelings matter. I am hereby validating them, so own that weepy clinginess. If you were happy about your daughter leaving, I'd be worried about you."

Janet swiped at damp lashes with a chuckle then changed the subject. "Did you bring the Girl Scout book?"

"It's in my car."

"I think it would be the perfect distraction."

"Say no more." Debbie got up and walked down the steps to the driveway. Hot air rushed out of her little red Toyota when she opened the door. She picked up the green book and the padded envelope containing their finds. Everything but the flower that still sat on her closet shelf.

If nothing else came from searching for answers to the questions Roxanne Britton's book roused, she would at least know more than she'd ever expected to about the pretty, poisonous flower. She hadn't been able to find any information on whether the toxins in monkshood were still active after the plant had dried, but she had learned that it was a part of the *Aconitum* species, so named because aconitine was one of the neurotoxins found in the plant. The Latin name came from the Greek ἀκόνιτον, which translated to "without struggle." Experts believed that, since it was used as a poison on arrowheads and acted so quickly, the name probably derived from its victims falling without a struggle.

She'd also read about a gardener whose cause of death was recorded as "unknown causes," but his father was convinced he had simply brushed monkshood while on the job. It certainly wasn't something to mess with.

She joined Tiffany, Ashling, and Janet at the glass-topped wicker coffee table on the porch.

Tiffany indicated the book. "Mom told us a little about some stuff you found in that."

Debbie handed it to her. "It was on display at the depot earlier this year. Scouts did a lot to help the war effort in the forties, including volunteering at the depot. I thought there might be some nice old-school stuff for Ashling. Turns out there was a lot more than that."

Tiffany carefully opened the book. "Is my old Girl Scout book still around?"

"I'm sure it's still upstairs in your shrine—I mean, room," Janet joked.

They laughed.

"I know for sure ours weren't nearly this thick," Tiffany said, handing the book to her friend.

"We didn't have the internet for additional information then. They probably had to put everything in the book." She flipped to the back. "This has 694 pages. Can you believe it?"

"There must be a veritable treasure trove of information in there," Debbie said. "And we've barely scratched the surface."

Ashling opened to the table of contents. "There are ten program fields. Arts and Crafts, Community Life, Health and Safety, Homemaking, International Friendship, Literature and Dramatics, Music and Dancing, Nature, The Out-of-Doors, and Sports and Games. Wow." She grinned at them. "We'll have fun with this."

Debbie opened the envelope and laid the items within it on the table. She told them about the monkshood, and Tiffany read the index card out loud. She frowned. "Why would someone keep something so dangerous?"

"Your guess is as good as mine," Debbie told her.

For the next half hour, questions and theories filled the air, with no real answers in sight.

When they seemed to have exhausted all possibilities, they moved on to talk of Ashling's plans. "One of the first things I want to do is plan an overnight at Camp Saundustee," she explained. "Tiff and I have so many great memories from there."

A wistful expression made Tiffany's eyes shine. "Like that raccoon eating your strawberry lip gloss, and the night the lights went out and we ate dinner in the dark. Oh! Remember the girl whose soda can was full of bees, and they had to rush her to the ER?"

Ashling rolled her eyes. "That girl was me."

"Hey." Tiffany straightened. "We should go out to Saundustee now. Campers leave by noon on Sunday. The place should be empty."

"We should probably call first," Debbie said.

Janet pulled out her phone. "I have the number. I made cakes for the camp's seventy-fifth anniversary a couple years ago." She started the call then put it on speaker.

"Camp Saundustee. This is Sara. How may I help you?"

Janet's eyes lit. "Sara Loring?"

"Yes."

"Hi, Sara. This is Janet Shaw. I heard you were the new director. Haven't seen you in…"

Janet's words faded into the heavy air as the name she'd repeated pressed into Debbie's chest like a fist. She knew of only one person in the world who had every reason to never want to hear the name Debbie Albright ever again—much less see her face.

Sara Loring.

Dennison, Ohio
May 29, 1942

Caroline was in a mood. Roxy sped ahead of her on her bicycle, catching up with Minnie, whose pretty pink baubles bounced at the end of her two thick braids as she pedaled hard. She felt a twinge of guilt for being the one to cause the mood, but Caroline would forgive her as soon as she had a chance to explain.

Yesterday afternoon, when they'd started talking about planning something for tonight, Caroline had launched into a list of people to invite. Roxy had interrupted with, "Let's keep this small. Just our closest friends."

Roxy's mom had always told her, "It's better to have a few close friends you know you can trust than a big circle of friends who don't really know you." They did have the bigger circle, but now was not the time. "I need you to trust me on this," she'd said. "I'll explain it all when we get to camp."

Caroline had acquiesced but not cheerfully. "This better be good," she growled. About halfway into their five-mile ride, she'd stopped talking to either of them.

Roxy shifted the pack on her back. The army-issued haversack had belonged to her grandfather. It had gone to France with him in 1917. The thick canvas was heavy even when it was empty. Filled with everything they needed for the task ahead, it was a miserable burden. Sweat trickled down her sides. She'd hoped Caroline would offer to carry the two-man tent the three of them would pile into. She hadn't, but then again, she had no idea how much extra weight Roxy carried.

When they reached the camp, they hid their bicycles behind the building that would eventually serve as the camp office. From what her father had told her, she knew the 250-acre parcel would be divided into units, most with tents but one with cabins. The wooden tent platforms had all been built, and now they waited for the canvas that would cover them and the girls who would fill them. Someday.

Roxy led Minnie and Caroline past the place where they usually camped. Minnie's brown eyes were wide with a mixture of both fear and excitement. "Humor me, please," Roxy said.

She led them along an overgrown path to a clearing. Surrounding the grassy area were five small cabins. Each had four walls, a wood floor, and an unshingled plywood roof. Window openings were covered with sheets of wood. Eventually, the cabins would contain *built-in bunks. The outhouse was completely finished, which she was glad to see.*

Roxy walked up the steps of the cabin closest to the outhouse. The door swung open with a gentle push, and she led her friends inside.

"What are we doing?" Minnie asked. "It's like an oven in here."

It was, and the slivers of sunlight painting stripes on the dirt-and-leaf-covered floor meant the roof wouldn't keep out the rain. Roxy shrugged off her pack and dumped it in a corner. "Let's sit outside, and I'll explain."

Minnie and Caroline took off their packs and joined her on the steps, one waiting with anticipation, the other with irritation.

"First, I need you to make a solemn promise that you won't repeat anything I'm going to tell you. Not to anyone. Do I have your word?"

Minnie's brows converged. "As long as we're not doing anything illegal."

How was she supposed to answer that? Maybe by not answering. "We need to help someone, a friend of mine, who's in trouble."

Caroline glared. "What friend?"

"Jade."

"Your friend in California?" Minnie asked.

"Yes. She's in trouble, but not through any fault of her own."

"Because she's Japanese." Caroline didn't pose it as a question. Her face softened. "She's coming here, isn't she?"

"Yes. But no one can know. Do I have your word?" She aimed the question at Caroline. "Not anyone. Not even your parents."

"Especially not my parents." Caroline nodded. "I'm in." She gave a small smile. "And I'm sorry."

"Me too." Roxy nudged her shoulder. "I probably didn't have to be so secretive, but I was scared somebody might overhear us."

"Jade is our age, right?" Minnie asked. "And she's coming all the way from California? With her parents?"

"No."

Minnie's eyes widened. "Alone? How?"

"I have no idea."

"When is she coming?" Caroline asked.

"I don't know that either. She posted a letter five days ago. I'm guessing that's the day she left LA. I put a note on the front door telling her the back door is open in case she arrives while we're out here. I told her to hide in our basement and keep all the lights off, and that I'll be back soon."

"If my father—" Caroline began.

"I know. That's why we're here."

Her friends gaped at her. Minnie was the first to squeak, "Jade is going to live here?"

CHAPTER FIVE

Debbie sat in the passenger seat of Janet's car on the way to Camp Saundustee, wishing she could be excited about returning to the camp where she and Janet had made so many memories in junior high and high school. She wished she could enjoy hearing Tiffany and Ashling discuss their adventures.

But if it meant coming face-to-face with the woman whose family had left town because of what she'd failed to do thirty years ago, she'd rather do almost anything else.

True, she'd been fourteen, an age when girls are far more motivated by peer pressure than good judgment, but the memory still haunted her. She'd tried to find Sara on social media but hadn't been able to. Assuming she'd gotten married and her name had changed, Debbie had given up. Apparently, that wasn't the case.

"Why so quiet?" Janet asked over the hum of conversation and laughter in the back seat.

"Just thinking."

"Memories?" Janet grinned. "I've been thinking about the time we put all those tiny frogs in the pantry and the cook refused to make supper until the culprits confessed."

Debbie tried to smile. "We did some crazy stuff." But even Janet didn't know what she'd done to Sara.

The summer after eighth grade, Debbie had decided to change her image. She was tired of being one of the quiet, "nice" girls. She wanted to be one of the girls who had tons of friends and wasn't always afraid of doing something wrong. Camp was a good place to start. Even though she'd shared a tent with Janet as usual, there were plenty of opportunities to meet people from other schools and hang out with more popular girls. She'd hoped the other two girls in their tent would be more daring and adventurous than the group she usually hung out with.

They were. Bridgette and Hailey were from New Philadelphia. They were wild and funny, always talking about boys and the things they did at home when they snuck out after curfew. Debbie was drawn to them. In spite of Janet's warnings, she'd started acting and talking like them. For the first time ever, she was accepted by the cool girls.

Within the first week, she'd found out what that would cost. She'd have to choose between being accepted and doing the right thing. And she had to prove she belonged by being as catty as they were. Her first opportunity came when Sara Loring arrived five days late after being sick. And she stuttered. "Please be kind and considerate and include her," the counselor had said, looking directly at Janet and Debbie, likely sure she could count on them.

Sara lived in Dennison, but she was a year older than Debbie, so they didn't really know each other. Still, she should have felt some sense of responsibility. But the next day, when the popular girls started mocking Sara, intentionally stuttering when they said her name, Debbie had laughed along with them. It wasn't until she'd found Sara sobbing in the bathroom that the impact of their words sank in and made her feel sick to her stomach.

From then on, she'd made it a point to be kind to Sara, and she'd distanced herself from the "cool" girls. When the camp director had moved Bridgette and Hailey to another craft group and put Sara in their place, Debbie had gone overboard to sound enthusiastic. But the damage was done. When school started, she learned that Sara's family had moved out of state because Sara was having "emotional issues."

As an adult, she'd been able to understand that she was likely not the source of all of Sara's problems, but the thought that she had contributed to them still left her with regret.

With a fortifying deep breath and a prayer for grace, she participated in the conversation about camp memories until they reached the camp entrance. When Janet parked in front of Reese Hall, the building that housed the offices and a large meeting room, Debbie wiped her damp palms on her capri pants and opened the door. She was glad they'd all taken the time to change out of their church clothes, but her nerves were the main thing she felt.

"Sara said they have maps," Janet said. "They've added some buildings since you girls were here, and it's definitely different than what Debbie and I remember."

Debbie tried to tell herself it was silly to be so nervous over a mistake she'd made thirty years ago, but her nerves still jangled. *Lord, let me be humble. Help me to know if an apology is needed, or if that would merely serve to open old wounds.* Yet those old wounds must have healed, and it made her curious. What had happened in Sara's life that would allow her to come back to a place where she'd suffered so much pain?

The woman sitting behind the counter was not Sara. Debbie had expected her to be there to greet them. She breathed a quiet sigh of relief then had second thoughts. Wouldn't it be better to get this meeting over with, maybe put to rest decades of bad feelings on both sides…Sara's hurt and Debbie's guilt?

As Janet stepped up to ask for a map, Debbie joined the younger women in chatting about the old photographs lining the walls. The first black-and-white photo showed a group of nine people, men and women. The woman in the middle held a shovel. Her foot was raised, resting on the top of the blade. The caption read, *Groundbreaking. April 1941. Construction was halted when the US entered the war and did not resume until 1946.* The next showed a group of girls in matching shorts and blouses standing in front of a platform tent. It was titled *Opening Day. June 8, 1947.*

"Interesting." Debbie murmured under her breath, but it caught Ashling's attention.

"What's interesting?"

"According to the dates in Roxy's handbook, she would never have attended camp here. She turned fifteen in 1941, so she would have been your age when the camp opened. I guess I assumed she would have gotten the flower near Jupiter's Helm."

"Where the cave is?"

Debbie nodded. "We found out Jupiter's Helm is another name for monkshood."

"I always pictured the mythical god of the sky standing on top of that hill calling down thunder and lightning," Tiffany said. "But you think it was named for the flower? Or the other way around?"

"I think it's possible. It's also possible I'm overthinking."

While waiting for Janet, who was carrying on an animated conversation with the woman at the desk, they circled the room, moving through the decades. When they reached 1992, Debbie scanned the group photos. The camp hosted four two-week sessions every summer. It wasn't hard to find the one she and Janet had attended. A hand-painted banner strung between two trees hung above a group of close to two hundred girls. The sign read, GIRL SCOUT CAMP 1992.

Debbie peered closer at the photo, then gasped.

"Did you find you and Mom?" Tiffany asked.

All Debbie could do was nod. She and Janet stood in the front row—with a smiling Sara between them. When was the picture taken? Not the first day of camp, since Sara hadn't been there. But it couldn't have been after the teasing had started.

Numbly, she followed Tiffany to the more recent photos and listened to their giggles as they talked about their hairstyles and the girls they'd met at camp.

Janet approached with several papers in hand. "All set. I told her we were curious about what the camp was like in the forties, so she made a copy of one of the original layout blueprints."

"Good." Debbie kept her eyes on a door behind the front desk. "Is Sara going to meet us somewhere?"

"Sorry. I should have mentioned that after I talked to her on the phone. She had to leave as soon as the last camper was picked up. She was heading out to visit family in Minnesota and won't be back until Saturday. I told her the three of us should get together for coffee sometime."

Debbie answered with a weak smile. She'd face that another day. For now, she could let her shoulders lower to their normal position. As they stepped outside, she felt every muscle in her body relax. The apology was probably needed and was certainly merited, but it wouldn't happen today.

Janet held up the map. "Since everything's laid out in a big semi-circle, let's start here and go counterclockwise. We can stop at anything we want to check out. Personally, I'm wondering if the tents in Hickory Haven still have the same platforms. Debbie and I carved our initials and our current crushes on the floor under our beds."

Tiffany feigned shock. "Mother! Do you know what you would have said to me if you'd heard I did something like that?" She grinned at Ashling. "Or something like pulling nails out of a tent platform in Cloud Crest so we could nail our flip-flops twenty feet up in an oak tree."

"Daughter!" Janet mirrored Tiffany's playful tone. "How could you?"

"That was our most creative exploit, wasn't it?" Ashling winked at Tiffany. "Of course, there were all of the traditional things like injecting blue food coloring into our counselor's toothpaste."

"I think I'm supposed to scold you, but that's actually funny, since it's mostly harmless," Janet said.

They passed the Maple Bluff unit, since none of them had stayed in it. As they reached Hickory Haven, the one where she and Janet had stayed every year they'd gone to camp, Debbie felt a rush of nostalgia. If she could blot out the memories of what she'd done to Sara, the rest was good. So many friendships made, so many adventures. It was here she'd learned to kayak and build a fire. She still had a huge repertoire of camp songs in her head.

Janet ducked into the tent they'd stayed in that final year, then popped her head out a minute later. "The floors have been sanded. We've been erased, Debbie."

If only some memories could be so easily eradicated.

Ashling bumped her shoulder. "Penny for your thoughts?"

Debbie laughed. "Lost in the past. I was trying to remember all the words to the Promise and Law." It wasn't the whole truth, but the thought had crossed her mind when they entered the unit.

"Ooh. I need the practice. Let's say the promise together."

"'On my honor, I will try: To serve God and my country, to help people at all times, and to live by the Girl Scout Law,'" they chorused then grinned at each other.

Janet and Tiffany joined them, and the two younger women recited the Girl Scout Law. Debbie listened carefully because she knew the wording had changed since her days in the scouts.

"'I will do my best to be honest and fair, friendly and helpful, considerate and caring, courageous and strong, and responsible for what I say and do, and to respect myself and others, respect authority, use resources wisely, make the world a better place, and be a sister to every Girl Scout.'"

How had her fourteen-year-old self been able to recite that creed every day right after the Pledge of Allegiance and still been able to join in on taunting Sara for the sake of popularity? She thought of Greg's boys and the girls Ashling would lead. Maybe after she made things right with Sara, hers was a story she needed to share.

Janet had apparently been thinking along similar lines. "Remind me of the 'responsible for what I say and do' part if Gastro Gnome surfaces again."

"I'll need that reminder too," Debbie agreed.

As they walked around the circle of canvas-covered tents, something about the configuration struck Debbie. The eight tents weren't arranged in a perfect circle. Because of trees or massive rocks, some were up to eight feet farther back than others. She kept the theory this sparked to herself. The next unit might help her decide if her hunch was right.

They left Hickory Haven, chatting the whole way about the girls they'd met and their favorite counselors. They reached a narrow path, where a wooden signpost directed them to Jupiter's Helm.

When they found the small creek, Janet said, "This is spring fed. I remember our counselor, Belle, telling us about it one year."

"The stream seems a lot smaller," Debbie said. "I wonder if that little waterfall still exists."

"It's on the way to Jupiter's Helm, right? Around that bend?"

"It should be." As they followed the stream around the base of a hill, Debbie caught the sound of running water. In moments, they stood in front of a ten-foot-high waterfall, its spray sparkling in the sunlight.

"Um, Mom?" Tiffany held back a tangle of vines with her right hand and pointed with her left. Underneath was a wooden sign with two words carved into it.

Jade's Shower

CHAPTER SIX

I don't remember ever seeing this before," Debbie said. "Do any of you?"

The others shook their heads. As Tiffany held the vines out of the way so Ashling could snap photos, Janet said, "It's old. Maybe it's been covered by foliage for decades and somebody finally cut it all back."

Debbie studied. "Jade's not a common name. Maybe Roxy never went to camp here, but we have reason to believe she was here, and she had a friend named Jade. But why not call it Jade's Falls?"

"The more you question, the more you learn," Janet said. It was a quote from one of her T-shirts. "But we're here for fun, not just clues. Let's go check out Jupiter's Helm."

The path along the stream narrowed, and Debbie took up the rear. She still hadn't shaken the dark cloud that fell over her when Janet first mentioned Sara's name, but Janet was right. They were here to have fun. She forced her mind to focus on the beauty around her.

Sunlight filtered through towering red maples, white oak, and eastern white pines, leaving soft patterns on the needle-strewn path. Up ahead, a patch of purple caused her breath to hitch. As they drew nearer, she recognized the feathery blossoms—asters, in a swath as large as her living room. Their purple heads were raised to greet the sunlight, swaying in a gentle breeze. Backed by the sound of the waterfall and the trickle of spring water flowing over polished rocks, the scene created an almost tangible sense of tranquility.

Ashling stopped and took a picture. "It's so peaceful. I can't wait to bring the girls out here. I met a couple who moved from Pittsburgh a week ago. They have fifteen-year-old twin girls, and I hope they'll want to join my troop. They've spent their entire lives in a downtown apartment complex and have never been camping, never even sat around a campfire. I can't wait to watch their reactions when they see this."

Debbie caught up to her. "You're going to be so good for them, and the rest of the local girls."

Ashling's freckled cheeks grew pink. "Thank you. It's a scary responsibility. For some girls it'll simply be fun stuff to do once a week, but for others…" Tears sparkled in her eyes.

"Others like you?" Debbie prompted.

"Yes. I don't think most teachers, coaches, or scout leaders realize what a huge impact they can have on a kid with an absent parent. If my grandma, Janet, and a couple of Girl Scout leaders hadn't taken me under their wings, I'd probably have followed in my mom's footsteps. Of course"—she gave a bitter laugh—"a person has to actually be in your life for you to follow in their steps."

Debbie felt her heart squeeze. Ashling had been raised by her grandmother since she was young. Her mother had been out of the picture most of her life, due to a series of bad decisions and disastrous relationships. "What's the latest with your mom?"

Ashling sighed. "She's in rehab again. Visits and phone calls don't always go well, so I've started writing to her. I want to keep in touch with her, but it's better if the circumstances are controlled."

"Good for you," Debbie said. "It's not easy to keep showing love after someone disappoints you so many times, but you may be touching your mom in a way you won't know for years."

When Ashling started walking again, Debbie fell in line behind her. If she'd been blessed with a daughter, she'd want her to have a tender heart like Ashling's. At Ashling's age, she had pictured life in her early forties much differently than it had come out. Back then, she'd been in love with a handsome soldier stationed in Afghanistan. Their letters were filled with dreams and promise. They'd decided what kind of house they wanted and even named the two boys and two girls they would have. The reality that she would never have a daughter was sometimes hard, but God had put Tiffany and Ashling in her life for a reason. Maybe for such a time as this—to be a guide and mentor.

A verse from the sixteenth chapter of Proverbs had taken on a whole new meaning after Reed was killed: "In their hearts humans plan their course, but the Lord establishes their steps." In the early throes of her grief, the verse had haunted her. Now, years later, she could read it with a sense of peace. There were questions that would never be answered this side of heaven, but she was in a place of acceptance now. God had been beside her each step of the way as she walked down that difficult path. She loved this part of her journey and the glimpses of a promising future. God had not blessed her with a daughter, but it seemed he was preparing her heart to be loved again and to be a mom to two boys.

It wasn't until the moss-covered sandstone walls began to rise higher on each side of the winding stream that Debbie remembered what lay ahead. Right before the next bend, a rock-strewn path led up to the left. "Was it always this steep?" she whispered to Janet.

Janet groaned. "Pretty sure it wasn't. Must be erosion or something. It's definitely not that we have changed."

"Definitely not." Debbie flexed her arms then sighed. "I knew I should have joined a gym when I moved back."

"We've got this. Show no weakness to the youngsters," Janet whispered.

Fortunately, the ground was not muddy, and there were roots and vines to grab on to as they climbed the twenty-plus feet to the top. All the way, Debbie chanted to herself, *I think I can. I think I can. I think I can.*

The older, wiser women were slightly winded when they reached the top, but the difficulty was forgotten the moment they spotted the cave entrance.

The opening was surrounded by wildflowers—black-eyed Susans and coneflowers, purple asters and bright red cardinal flowers. It wasn't hard to imagine a patch of beautiful purple monkshood in the mix.

Cold air rushed from inside the cave. About six feet high and eight feet wide, the entrance yawned like a dragon's mouth. Debbie had heard that early settlers believed many of Ohio's caves were the gaping mouths of terrifying netherworld creatures. She had visited Ohio Caverns in West Liberty several times and could understand the idea. The stalactites and stalagmites easily brought to mind vicious teeth that may have frightened the first visitors, who hadn't had the advantage of electric lights throughout. The cave under Jupiter's Helm only ran about forty feet deep and, if she remembered right, was fairly level and not filled with anything resembling teeth.

Tiffany stopped before stepping inside. "We always had to pause here for a lecture from one of the counselors about not touching the walls."

"'And do not even think about leaving your initials.'" Ashling made her voice sound like a strict old librarian. Debbie hoped they'd never had a counselor with that shrill tone. "'The markings you will see were left by people who didn't yet have our understanding of the need to preserve our environment.'"

"People like us," Janet said with a laugh. "Pretty sure our initials are in here."

Using the flashlights on their phones, they stepped into the chilly, dark, damp space. The wet walls glistened. A few feet in, outside noises became muffled. Their soft footfalls and a constant, rhythmic dripping were the only sounds. A drop of water landed on Debbie's nose, and she grinned. Halfway in, they began to see names, dates, and symbols carved or painted on the walls.

"Reminds me of our depot bench," Janet said.

Debbie nodded. The wooden bench outside the café had been there since 1943. In the past eighty years, residents and visitors had carved hearts and initials on it until there was very little unmarked space. The iconic piece of Dennison history seemed meant for that, but it would have been a shame if human hands had destroyed this bit of God's creation. "I'm glad they never opened this to the public."

"Aren't there supposed to be some Native American petroglyphs in here?" Ashling asked.

"On the ceiling somewhere," Janet answered. "I remember joking about how they must have been eight feet tall to put drawings up there."

"There. I think." Tiffany pointed her phone at a spot high above their heads.

They combined their beams, creating a concentrated spotlight. Goose bumps rose on Debbie's arms.

"Is that…?" Janet didn't need to finish. A chunk of rock was missing where there had once been numbers, but Debbie definitely recognized the symbols.

マタイ

As they drove home, Ashling created a message group for the four of them and sent the pictures she'd taken of the sign and in the cave. When her phone dinged, Debbie enlarged the picture of the Matthew symbols. "Good shot, Ashling."

"Thank you. I wonder if there ever were petroglyphs, or if someone saw these symbols and thought they must have been made by indigenous people."

"It's possible. Though not if there were numbers next to it."

"True."

"You're assuming Jade was the same age as Roxy, right?" Tiffany asked.

Debbie swiveled to face the back seat. "Yes. But that's making some big assumptions. We have the date they went to see Mrs. Miniver at the State Theater. June of 1942. We know Roxy was fifteen at the time. It's a guess that 'M' and 'C' and 'J' were her friends, and that 'J' was Jade. I could be wrong on that. I'm also going on the assumption that she would only have used the Girl Scout book until she was eighteen, so it seems reasonable to think that everything we found stuck in it was put there between September of 1941 and spring of '44 or '45 when she would have graduated from high school."

"All during the war," Ashling said. "When the camp wasn't open."

Tiffany sighed. "What's the thing you said about questions, Mom?"

"The more you question, the more you learn. That's a quote from my home economics teacher. She's the one who taught me to love baking. When we opened the café, there were so many areas where Debbie and I were clueless. I had Mrs. Twining's words printed on a T-shirt so I'd quit thinking my questions were too dumb to ask."

"Questions are about all we've got right now," Debbie said. "Which reminds me. I shoved one into the back of my brain about an hour ago, and it got buried. Where's the map and the blueprint?"

Janet pointed to her purse, on the floor by Debbie's feet. "Outside pocket."

Debbie reached down and pulled out the map and the photo-copy of a blueprint probably made by an architect in the forties. The block-printed labels were all underlined and appeared too precise to have been done by an amateur. The original rendering was likely much, much larger, and possibly the first page in a series of sketches.

The bird's-eye view showed a building labeled *Main Office Building*. Though it was square, it had to be the original structure that was now the L-shaped Reese Hall. Next to that was a unit con-sisting of five cabins. Arranged in a semicircle around the bluff overlooking the valley were other camping units, each with eight permanent tents and its own latrine.

Letters in the bottom right-hand corner of the photocopied blueprint caught her attention. A name.

Eric R. Britton

Dennison, Ohio
May 30, 1942—Memorial Day

"Time to pack up. We've got a parade to get to."

Exhausted groans answered Roxy's forced cheeriness on Saturday morning. They'd been up and working since first light.

"I can't possibly walk the whole parade mile," Caroline moaned, but there was something in her voice that belied her woeful words, something Roxy hadn't heard in a long time. Pride.

Roxy put her father's hammer and drill in her backpack. She wrapped the handsaw in a towel then stood in the cabin doorway, rubbing her right shoulder and smiling. "We did good."

Her bedraggled friends nodded. "We did," Caroline agreed.

The floor had been swept with a broom Minnie made from brush tied to a straight pine branch, then washed by Caroline on her hands and knees. Minnie, the only one of them with no fear of heights, had offered to finish the roof. "I have no idea what I'm doing," she'd said, "but I'm pretty sure I can figure out how to keep the rain out."

On one end of the single room sat Roxy's handiwork, a bed made of weathered two-by-fours. "Thanks, Dad," Roxy murmured under her breath.

Her father was not only an architect. He'd also been a Hollywood set builder and partner in the family construction business. When Roxy turned ten, he'd started the tradition of taking her out for doughnuts on Saturday mornings. Then they'd visit his current jobsite before any of his workers arrived, and he'd teach her how to use hand tools. She loved the smell of fresh-cut pine, and the way curlicues snaked out of a hole as she slowly rotated the handle on a drill.

When she was old enough to be trusted with a saw, she'd made her first piece of furniture, a small table much like the one that now sat in the middle of the room and would serve as Jade's dining and workspace.

"We have a kerosene lamp in the attic," Minnie said. "And there's a box of dishes that used to belong to my great-grandma. I don't think anyone even remembers they're there."

"Our linen closet is full of sheets. Way more than we need," Caroline said. "My mom will never miss one set. And I bet I could make a mattress out of…"

Roxy's eyes suddenly stung. It would take a miracle to make this happen, to keep Jade safe until her mother got home. But she was witnessing a miracle right here and now. "Thank you." Her words came out hushed and rough, and her friends immediately wrapped their arms around her. She grinned at them. "Too bad there isn't a Girl Scout badge for harboring fugitives."

CHAPTER SEVEN

The sun was low and golden on the horizon, casting long shadows across Janet and Ian's backyard as they sat around the wicker table, munching on oatmeal scotchies and researching. Five people, five phones, searching up everything they could think of relating to Camp Saundustee and Eric R. Britton.

Ranger the gray cat curled on Tiffany's lap, and Laddie the terrier lay under Debbie's chair. Both jumped when Ian yelled, "Bingo!" But his excitement died as quickly as it came. "Not our guy. This Eric Britton lived in California. He designed private homes and also worked as a set designer in Hollywood."

"That's weird," Debbie said. "I wouldn't have guessed that there would be more than one Eric Britton during that time. But I guess anything is possible."

Ian kept scrolling. "Wait, there's a newspaper article here. Listen. 'MGM is losing one of the best set designers of this decade. Eric R. Britton's sleek, geometric designs have brought small towns and panoramic city views to life for movie lovers, and inspired art deco buildings throughout the country for the past decade. It is with a heavy heart that we bid goodbye to this architectural genius and wish him the best as he moves to the Midwest to assist with the family construction firm that gave him his start. The executive board of

MGM wishes him a fond farewell—and, if rumors are to be believed, a substantial incentive for his return as soon as possible.'"

"So our Roxy might have been related to someone who once worked in Hollywood," Debbie mused. "I'm texting Greg to see if he ever heard of our guy, though he saw the scout handbook and the name Britton didn't seem to ring any bells."

"I'll text Ellie," Janet said. "I'll tell her it isn't urgent, but I know she loves digging into local stories."

Debbie had found Ellie Cartwright, head librarian at the Claymont Library, to possess a wealth of state and local historical knowledge. "Good idea."

Tiffany raised her hand. "I think I found a few things on a newspaper archives app. This one mentions his family. It's from 1939. 'After the passing of longtime resident Harvey Washburn, many thought his daughter and son-in-law would return to California, but the chamber is thrilled to announce that Eric and Luanne Britton and their two daughters have chosen to make Dennison their home. The Brittons have sold Washburn Construction, and Eric will resume his career as an architect, opening an office in his home. The Dennison Chamber of Commerce invites you to an open house at the Britton residence, 626 Grant Street, from two o'clock to four o'clock on Sunday, April 16.'"

"That's Roxy's address," Debbie said. "She must be one of the daughters."

Tiffany sat back in her chair. "How old would Roxy have been?"

"Twelve. She would have turned thirteen in September of 1939."

Debbie's phone alerted her to a new text from Greg. CAN'T THINK OF ANY ART DECO BUILDINGS IN THE COUNTY. I'M SEARCHING THE CHAMBER DATABASE FOR THE NAME ERIC BRITTON. ROXY'S FATHER?

THAT'S OUR CURRENT THEORY, she replied.

Greg's answer came in seconds. IF ROXY'S DAD DESIGNED CAMP SAUNDUSTEE, IT MAKES SENSE THAT SHE MIGHT HAVE SPENT TIME THERE, GATHERING FLOWERS, ETC. MIND IF I COME JOIN YOU? IT'LL BE EASIER TO COMPARE NOTES IN PERSON, AND I ALWAYS LIKE AN EXCUSE TO SEE YOU.

Debbie glanced up to find everyone staring at her. "What?"

"What's with the smile?" Janet asked, the corners of her own lips curving. "Are art deco buildings that beautiful?"

Heat rose into Debbie's cheeks. "Greg mentioned that it might be easier to consult him if he were actually here."

"Invite him," Ian said at once. "We'll probably get even more done with him here."

"Definitely," Janet agreed firmly. "Tell him that if he hurries, he might even get a cookie."

Ian scooped up the plate. "Hey, no one said I would have to share my wife's baking. Now I'm not sure I want him to come."

Laughing, Janet swatted his arm while Debbie texted Greg the invite.

Rolling her eyes at her parents' antics, Tiffany got the conversation back on track. "What did you say earlier about sticking something in the back of your brain, Debbie? Can you unstick it?"

"I almost forgot about that." She dug in her purse for the maps.

Janet's phone dinged. "Ellie answered. She said she's going to go over to the library to start searching the archives. And she thanked me for giving her something to do on a boring Sunday afternoon. In that case, what else should we ask about? Roxanne Britton and somebody named Jade for sure."

"Anything about the stolen sugar," Debbie suggested.

When Janet finished the text, she said, "Okay, back to that thing stuck in your brain. Is it unstuck now?"

"It is." Debbie laid the photocopied blueprint on the table then pulled out the fake constellation chart. "I think I might have figured out what the constellation map really is." She grinned at their expectant faces. "But I'm not saying a word until Greg gets here."

While waiting for Greg, Debbie came up with an idea. She asked Janet and Tiffany if they had any dry-erase markers.

Tiffany jumped up. "There are some in the craft cupboard. I'll get them."

By the time she returned, Greg's truck was pulling up in front of the house. After Greg joined the circle, lemonade in hand and Hammer at his feet, Debbie asked them all to take their drinks and cookies off the table and close their eyes.

"Do we need to start a drumroll?" Ian asked.

"In a minute. First, I need to concentrate. And not break anything."

"Break?" Janet echoed. "All you've got is markers and paper."

"Shh." Debbie reached under the tabletop and found finger spaces in the wicker, then gently pushed up on the glass top until she could slide the constellation chart beneath it. Then she traced the lines, copying the stars onto the glass. When she finished, she said, "Drumroll, please. Now you may open your eyes."

Greg, sitting to her left, leaned over to study her work. "Clever. But what's it for?"

"You'll see." Using the same technique, she lifted the glass half an inch, pulled out the star chart, and replaced it with the reduced-size architectural rendering. While the scale didn't match perfectly, it was close enough to produce four gasps of realization.

The lines in the "constellations" connected tents, represented by stars. "HH stands for Hickory Haven," Janet said, a bit of awe in her voice.

Debbie moved the paper so the second set of stars and lines matched up with the tent circle in Cloud Crest. When she moved it again, it was clear the third grouping represented cabins in Maple Bluff.

Tiffany sat with her mouth slightly ajar. "HH, CC, and MB. Why didn't we think of that before?"

"Way cool," Ashling said. "So the red stars are each on a cabin or tent, but I wonder what they signify. We were out there and didn't see anything special about those particular things."

"What if it was a game?" Tiffany suggested. "A treasure hunt maybe?"

Debbie nodded. "Could be. It may not have anything to do with anything else in the guidebook."

"Or it could," Ian said. "I think another trip to the camp is in order. And I'd like to join you, if possible."

"That sounds fun to me too," Greg added. "But I don't want to intrude."

Debbie smiled at him. "You never intrude. You are always welcome."

"Speak for yourself," Janet teased.

Ashling pulled something out of her back pocket. "I grabbed a couple of brochures. Figured I better familiarize myself with the changes at camp. In the offseason, which started today, they rent out cabins for family reunions and retreats. I think we should organize an overnight stay."

"I'd enjoy that, maybe with my sons," Greg said. "Maybe we could earn a Star Finder badge of our own."

Ashling grinned. "I could make badges for you. The camp would be a great place for stargazing, away from city lights. Wait. I read something about that in the current Girl Scout handbook." She tapped on her phone. "Here it is. 'Host a star party. Organize a stargazing event for Girl Scouts and friends and family. Bring a star chart and flashlights. Trace some constellations. Find the Big Dipper. Invite an astronomer to give insight.' I could make this an actual Girl Scout event."

"I'm just an amateur astronomer, but if we planned it soon, we could catch some of the Perseid meteor shower," Greg said. "We could probably see it on any clear night, but it will be best in a little over a week. I suppose it would have to be on a Friday or Saturday night even though school's out. So what about next Saturday? Selfishly, that works great for me, but the boys will be at a church lock-in until—" He stopped. "Sorry. I realize I'm kind of inviting myself."

"The handbook says friends and family. You fall under the friend category, Mr. Connor, and you're more of an astronomer than any of the rest of us," Ashling said. "I would like to open it to the girls and one parent or guardian. And, of course, our mentors and maybe the Chief of Police."

"The church picnic is at noon the next day," Janet reminded them. "I'm in charge of organizing desserts. I suppose I could leave camp early though."

"Let's say we're done by ten thirty. That'll give us time for breakfast and maybe a hike on Sunday morning. We'll all be too tired for anything else." Ashling held up the brochure. "Tents or cabins?"

"Cabins," Debbie said. "In case we have some girls who'd rather not rough it—or parents. I had a couple of coworkers in Cleveland who thought a hotel room without a hot tub was rustic living. Cabins are a bit less primitive than tents."

"Good thinking," Ashley agreed. "I'll see if Maple Bluff is available. There are five cabins with six bunk beds in each. We could have up to thirty people, but it's short notice so I doubt we'll have that many."

"That's okay," Greg said. "I have two telescopes, and I might be able to borrow a couple more. The smaller the group, the more access they'll have to them, which means they'll learn more."

Debbie didn't bother to restrain the smile Greg's enthusiasm elicited. With the responsibility of running his own construction business and serving as chamber president while raising two boys on his own, there were times when the weight of it all seemed heavy on his shoulders. It was nice to see this excitement lighting his eyes.

"I'm hoping some of the girls will use this to start earning their badges." Ashling scrolled on her phone. "There are five requirements: Watch the skies during morning, afternoon, and evening, and take note of changes. Investigate the science of sky by watching a video. Explore the connection between people and flight. Help clear sky pollution. And finally, create sky art."

"I've always appreciated the educational aspect of Girl Scouts," Janet said. "It's such a well-rounded approach that makes sure there's something for every kind of learner."

Ashling flipped through the vintage scout handbook. "Maybe I'll also take the girls through some of the historical requirements for earning the Star Finder badge. There are fourteen listed. 'Make a sky map showing the location of the constellations you have…'" She squinted. "There are smudges all over these pages, so it's hard to read some of them. Ah, the rest of that line is, 'you have chosen to learn. Make something other than a map to help people learn about stars. Learn all you can about some of the most famous discoveries made at observatories.'" She glanced up at Greg. "I belonged to an astronomy club in high school. We took a trip to the Warren Rupp Observatory in Bellville. Have you been there, Mr. Connor?"

"Yes, and it's great. There's also the Swasey Observatory in Granville. There's a planetarium at the Wilderness Center in Wilmot that puts on some great programs. The boys and I went to a few last fall, and we loved them."

"Me too! They also do a star watch every month, kind of like what we're going to do. They provided telescopes, or we could bring our own. I went with some of my astronomy geek friends once, and I bet it would be a great thing for the Girl Scouts to do too. I was there on a perfectly clear night, and we could see the rings of Saturn so vividly and moon craters that—" She stopped, blushing. "Sorry. I get a little too passionate sometimes."

Debbie put a hand on Ashling's shoulder. "No apologies. The girls you'll be leading need passionate role models. As Harriet Tubman said, 'Always remember, you have within you the strength, the patience, and the passion to reach for the stars to change the world.' I think you'll embody that for your scouts, and that's a great lesson for them to learn."

CHAPTER EIGHT

$\mathcal{E}$llie called," Janet said as Debbie zipped past her midmorning on Monday, two plates in one hand and a coffeepot in the other. "She's wondering if we can come to the library at four today."

"Of course we can," Debbie answered over her shoulder. "Assuming we've slowed down by then."

Closing time was two. Janet laughed.

The café had been buzzing all morning. After delivering the order, Debbie paused to take a drink of water and lean on the counter so she could catch her breath. A flash of shimmering auburn caught her eye, and she greeted Ashling. "Morning."

"Good morning." Ashling took the last open spot at the counter.

Paulette Connor, Greg's mother and an invaluable part-time café employee, set a napkin and silverware in front of her then hurried on to greet the next customers when the bell over the door dinged.

Debbie delivered a breakfast sampler to the man at the end of the counter then turned to Ashling. "The usual?"

"Someday I'm going to shock you and order something different, but for now, the usual, except I'd like the coffee iced, please."

"You got it."

As Debbie plated a chocolate-covered cake doughnut, Ashling said, "I called the camp this morning and booked Maple Bluff for

Saturday night." She reached into the bright orange shoulder bag that sat on her lap. "I couldn't sleep, so I made these last night. I've already sent emails to the girls in my troop." She handed several quarter-page flyers to Debbie. She'd found a watercolor painting of a log cabin under a starlit sky and put the information in a white box in the bottom left corner.

"You're good at this. You might want to add graphic design to your list of services for Jill of All Trades."

"Thanks. I love designing things. Hold that thought. I need to hand out a couple of these." She stood, and Debbie watched as she went to the door to meet the two teen girls walking in. Two identical teen girls. Probably the city kids who'd recently moved to town.

Debbie smiled as she watched the ease with which Ashling talked to the girls. She picked up two menus and was about to seat them when she realized there wasn't a single empty table.

And then she noticed something else. The door opened behind the girls, and a short woman with salt-and-pepper hair walked in. A woman she'd seen before.

"Grandma, this is Ashling Kelly," one of the girls said. "She's the Girl Scout leader. Ashling, this is our grandmother, Nomi Fairchild."

Debbie felt a cold dread wash over her as she stared at the unsmiling woman with huge hoop earrings and a shirt that said, Nomi Gnomes Best.

Love your enemies. Pray for those who persecute you. We'll get through this. She combined the verse the foreign exchange student had translated with Janet's words from Friday.

"Is that…?" Janet stood at Debbie's elbow, a platter of apple fritters in hand.

"Uh-huh. And we don't have an open table."

"Oh boy." Janet scanned the room. "Should we hurry someone along?"

Debbie gave a doleful laugh. "That'll help our ratings for sure, basically kicking out a regular."

Then she spotted Carly O'Sullivan, a frequent customer who had defended the café's honor in response to the review by Gastro Gnome, aka Nomi Fairchild. Carly was sitting with a friend who often accompanied her for a late breakfast on Mondays. Their plates were empty, but they were still nursing cups of coffee. "Be right back. You go give the gnome lady and her granddaughters menus." When Janet scowled, Debbie added, "With a smile, please."

After filling two to-go cups with coffee then grabbing two white bags and adding a fresh fritter to each, she approached Carly's table. "Good morning, ladies. Did you enjoy your breakfast?"

"Fantastic as always," Carly answered. Her friend nodded in agreement.

Debbie set the cups and bags on the table and picked up the empty plates. "I have a huge favor to ask." She turned to Carly, who was facing the front windows. "Janet and I would like to show our appreciation for your online support this past week, and we're wondering if you could help us out again." She looked pointedly toward the door.

Carly followed her gaze, and a smile broke out on her face. "We have to go now," she told her friend under her breath. "I'll explain when we get outside."

Both women stood with their to-go cups and fritters.

"Breakfast was wonderful as usual, Debbie," Carly announced to the dining room. "Can't find better service or coffee and pastry anywhere around. We'll be back next Monday." As she and her friend crossed the room, she called toward the kitchen, "Thanks, Janet. You make the best apple fritters in Ohio." At the door, she paused by the three customers waiting for a table. "Enjoy, ladies. It's the best gig in town."

Debbie bit down on her bottom lip as Paulette joined her in clearing off the table in record time. "Is that Gastro Gnome?" Paulette whispered.

"Yep."

"Well, you two work your cooking magic. I'll take the 'kill 'em with kindness' job."

Debbie laughed. "No one could do that job better than you."

Janet wiped the edge of the plate in Debbie's hand then repositioned a fan-cut strawberry. "I hope this will please Her Majesty."

Debbie did a final inspection of the beautifully presented omelet overflowing with meat and veggies and artfully sprinkled with sharp cheddar. The bacon strips framing it were expertly cooked to Gastro Gnome's specifications, and the English muffin toasted to perfection. "You've outdone yourself. I'll go first. Smile in place."

Paulette picked up two plates of golden-brown fluffy chocolate chip pancakes, and together they headed to the table where the two girls chatted and giggled while their grandmother typed on her tablet device.

"Welcome back to the Whistle Stop Café." Debbie infused her voice with all the cheerfulness she could muster. She set the plate in front of Nomi Fairchild at the best possible angle. "I hope you're all settling into your new home."

"We love it here," one girl said.

"Dennison is awesome," her sister added.

Nomi answered with a deadpan stare. "No use trying to butter me up. I've heard it all." She picked up her fork and prodded the omelet as if testing whether it were still alive. "Springy."

Debbie didn't dare make eye contact with Paulette. Was springy a good thing for an omelet? "Hope you enjoy it. I'll be back with a coffee refill in a minute."

"The pancakes smell so good," one of the girls said. The other nodded vigorously.

With a smile for both of them, Debbie pivoted.

"Hollandaise."

"Excuse me?" Debbie asked Nomi, who'd spoken.

"Hollandaise. That's what this needs."

The woman hadn't even taken a bite. Debbie breathed out a prayer on her controlled exhale. "You're right. That's exactly what it needs."

Scurrying to the kitchen, she rushed up to Janet and frantically whispered, "She wants hollandaise for the omelet."

"I'll separate the eggs."

Debbie crouched and dug out the immersion blender then fumbled and almost dropped the cord as she plugged it in. She didn't want to be afraid of this woman, but the stakes for the café were too high for her not to be nervous.

Opting for the fastest method, she cut a half-cup chunk of butter and plopped it into a glass measuring cup then stuck it in the microwave to melt. In no time, she was combining all of the ingredients except the butter. When she had a good emulsion, she drizzled in the melted butter, careful not to add it too quickly and risk cooking the eggs. Soon she had a perfectly smooth bright yellow sauce, which she poured into the small vintage pitcher Janet handed her.

Moments later, she was delivering the hollandaise to Nomi.

The critic squinted at the pitcher then at her watch, and then she cast a glance at Debbie and began to pour.

"That was fast," one of the twins said.

With a slight grimace likely meant as an apology for her grandmother, the other one added, "Thank you."

"You're welcome." Debbie smiled at the girls but aimed her words at Nomi as she took a bite and closed her eyes.

Debbie held her breath and waited. Was Nomi closing her eyes to savor the flavors, or to shut out the world so she could concentrate? When she finally opened them, she picked up her tablet and began typing. No eye contact with the person who had bent over backward to serve her every whim. With another smile at the girls, Debbie pivoted and walked to the counter.

"Did she like it?" Janet whispered.

"No clue."

For the next half an hour, she kept one eye on the Gastro Gnome table while seating customers and taking orders. Paulette was doing the same thing, keeping Nomi's coffee cup full and whisking away the girls' empty plates. Maybe they should thank the food critic for keeping them on their toes, since it seemed everything else in the café was operating even more smoothly and efficiently now that they were hypervigilant. Even their interactions with other guests were a bit more cheerful. And maybe a bit louder.

Finally, Nomi stood and picked up her tablet and purse. Debbie met her at the cash register. "Hope you enjoyed your meal." She gave Nomi her brightest smile.

Nomi nodded.

"Thank you for coming." Debbie addressed the girls. "I'm Debbie Albright, by the way, one of the owners."

To her surprise, both girls held out their hands. "I'm Macy, and this is Morgan."

Debbie shook both hands. "Ashling Kelly is a friend of mine. If you decide to join her troop, you'll be in for a real treat. Janet"—she motioned behind her, where Janet was pretending not to eavesdrop—"and I are planning on going to the stargazing event. I think it's going to be a lot of fun."

"I hope we can go," Morgan said. "We've never done anything like that."

Nomi shot her a glare. "For good reason. Like snakes and mosquitos and smoke."

Macy, a good head taller than her grandmother, gave a loud sigh. With another apologetic glance at Debbie, she said, "The pancakes were delicious. We'll be back soon." Then she waved and opened the door for Nomi.

Morgan didn't follow. "I suppose you know what my grandma wrote about the café."

Debbie nodded but tried not to show how she felt about the review.

"I'm sorry about that. She's mad because my dad made her move here with us. That wasn't about you, and I'm sorry if it hurts your business."

"I'll be praying for her."

The girl's eyes brightened. "Thank you. It might just take a miracle."

Dennison, Ohio
May 31, 1942

Walking out of church on Sunday morning, Roxy could hardly concentrate on Caroline's happy chatter. There was no explanation for the strange feeling that had haunted her since she'd opened her eyes this morning. Every muscle in her body hurt. Her nose and shoulders were sunburned. But it wasn't merely the aches and pains from yesterday's hard work that caused her sense of uneasiness.

Was this what her late grandmother would have called a nudge from the Lord? Roxy missed her grandmother dearly, but she had a whole collection of things she'd taught her. Her grandmother had explained to young Roxy that the nudge was "when you feel God telling you to pay attention."

Please, Lord, hold my attention where You need it to be. *As she said the silent prayer, a line from Jade's letter popped in her head.* I look forward to joining you for the Sunday church service you've told us about. *Was there a message in that sentence?*

Was Jade arriving today? The thought made her tingle with nerves. Mr. Davis would be home all day. She cringed at the thought of Jade walking up to her front door. Back in Los Angeles, no one would look twice at her, unless it was to admire her beauty. But here, in Dennison, Jade's long, glossy black hair and beautiful, dark almond-shaped eyes would make her stand out. If Caroline's father got even a glimpse of her, he'd...

Roxy couldn't let her thoughts go there. Instead, she focused on how wonderful it would be to have her closest friend back in her life. Of course, she'd never let Caroline know that was how she categorized Jade. Caroline was her best local friend, but she and Jade had once shared a playpen. As her mother and Aunt Miko often said, they were "second-generation best friends." Luanne and Miko were best friends who had co-owned a couture dress shop together in California. Jade and Roxy had been born four months apart and had grown up as sisters until Roxy's family moved to Ohio.

As they walked home from church, the feeling of heightened senses intensified. Her mother would call this afternoon, but the telephone was on the desk in the Davises' hallway. Could she somehow convey to her mother what was going on so that the Davises wouldn't catch on? Maybe she shouldn't tell her mother at all. It would make Luanne worry, which might lead her to talk to Mrs. Davis. That could spell disaster.

Then an idea hit. She turned to Caroline. "I think I'll go visit Aunt Dolly for a few minutes. Tell your parents I'll be home in time to help with dinner."

Aunt Dolly was her father's great-aunt. She was in her eighties and still lived in her own house, an odd-shaped, skinny two-story nearby. She had a live-in caretaker named Emma May, who appeared to be almost as old as Dolly herself.

Roxy breathed a relieved sigh when she saw the two women sitting on Aunt Dolly's front porch. This would give her the perfect vantage point. The narrow house sat on a hill two blocks from the train depot. From there, she would see a train arriving and might be able to meet Jade before she walked past the Davises' house to get to hers. If she was arriving today. There were fewer trains scheduled on Sunday, which would *make it easier to spot her friend. She'd picked up a schedule on Friday when she'd gone to the depot. The next was due in twenty minutes. Of course, she still had no idea how Jade was arriving. For all she knew, she might be hitchhiking and would come into town in the back of a pickup truck.*

The women were delighted to see her. As they sipped iced tea together, they asked her about the latest news from her parents and how she and her sister planned to spend the summer.

Right on time, the distant rumble of a train pierced the heavy air. Roxy finished her tea and was about to say her goodbyes when a man crossed the street toward them. "Enjoying the Lord's Day in style, I see, ladies." He doffed his hat, revealing a shock of tightly coiled white hair. William Franklin, Minnie's grandfather.

"Good morning, William," Emma May said. "Iced tea?"

"Don't mind if I do." He stepped onto the porch. "Haven't seen you in a long while, Roxy."

Emma May went into the house for another glass, and William settled into a wicker chair. Aunt Dolly said, "What's going on in the world today, William?" She turned to Roxy. "William reads three newspapers. We don't even need to listen to all the bad things on the radio because he gives us the headlines."

"Well, let's see, Hitler ordered all the Jews in Paris to wear a yellow star on their coats." His dark eyes clouded. "The commander of the German Reich Security Main Office was shot, and one of our subs sank a Japanese sub in the South China Sea."

Roxy stared into the distance. Her father could be in the South China Sea. "Here we sit, with cold beverages on a sunny day while there's so much evil in the world," she said.

Mr. Franklin nodded. "Always has been, always will be. Beauty and evil often live side by side. It's up to us to make sure we walk in wisdom and focus on the beauty."

"Hear, hear," Aunt Dolly agreed, lifting her glass.

Mr. Franklin thanked Emma May when she handed him a glass. "On the home front, four tons of sugar got stolen off a boxcar right here at the station during the night. With the rations, we'll probably see a lot more bootlegging and selling on the black market, just like in prohibition." He gave a loud sigh. "After I read those papers, I spend a good hour on my knees. It's all that helps to soothe my heart after."

"I hear you," Aunt Dolly said. "It's a sad thing when..."

Her words faded as Roxy spotted a woman walking up the hill, lugging a massive suitcase in each *hand. Sunlight glinted on blond bangs peeking out from a colorful scarf. Blond.*

But as the figure turned the corner, Roxy got a clear view of a large, shiny red purse. She'd been with Jade on their last family visit when she'd bought it. Jumping from her seat, she stammered an excuse and ran down the steps. She had to reach Jade before she got to the Brittons' house.

CHAPTER NINE

Debbie kicked off her shoes when she walked into the house on Monday afternoon and headed for the refrigerator. She'd made a pot of Earl Grey tea the "right" way this morning, not the microwave method she usually used. She'd recently seen it done on a British cooking show and was inspired by the methodical routine that had been performed for centuries.

While the water came to a boil on the stove, she'd filled a china teapot with hot water to warm it, and then she'd emptied it and wrapped it in a pretty floral tea cozy. When the kettle boiled, she'd poured the water over the tea in the pot and let it steep for exactly five minutes. She'd savored her perfect cup of morning tea while reading her daily devotional.

Hot tea was just the thing for greeting a summer sunrise. It was not the thing at all for a ninety-degree August afternoon. What she needed was the rest of that tea poured over a glass of ice and splashed with lemon juice.

Sinking onto her couch, she rested her aching feet on the coffee table. With an hour to relax until it was time to meet Ellie at the library, she picked up a George MacDonald novel Ian had loaned her. She loved the Scottish author's turn of phrase and romantic plots. She read two pages before she was interrupted by her phone. Kim's name flashed on the screen.

"Hi, Debbie. I couldn't remember where the old scout book came from, and I couldn't figure out why. But I finally realized it's because I wasn't here at the time. I asked the board if anyone knew anything about it, and Len Farnham said that he was putting up the Girl Scout display when Minnie Franklin brought it in for the exhibit. I never opened the book, and I doubt he did either."

"Thanks. This mystery keeps getting more and more interesting."

They ended the call, and Debbie picked up a pen to make a note. *Ask Harry about M.*

She stopped, staring at the letter. Was it possible Harry's cousin Minnie was the *M* written on the back of the theater ticket? Harry said she'd been a Girl Scout.

She finished the note to talk to Harry about Minnie then tried to get back to her book. But her brain had switched to investigation mode, so she opened a browser on her phone and typed in *Nomi Fairchild*. The options that came up caused her mouth to gape.

Restaurant Wins Defamation Suit Against Critic

Nomi Fairchild's Reign of Terror Has Ended

BAD Critic Loses BADly

BAD stood for *Big Apple Dining*, the magazine Nomi had worked for until a year ago when she was sued and lost. According to one source, she had needed to sell both of her homes to cover legal fees and still ended up bankrupt. Another said she "wasn't likely to be picked up by another magazine anywhere in the known world."

"No wonder she's angry." If she'd been forced to live with her son and his family because she'd lost everything, including her reputation, it wasn't surprising that she appeared angry and depressed.

However, Debbie soon discovered that losing her position and wealth hadn't stopped Nomi. In fact, the publicity had caused her blog following to grow exponentially.

The next article was Nomi's review of an up-and-coming farm-to-table restaurant. She'd titled it LEAVE IT ON THE FARM. Debbie read the words out loud in horror. "'As if the chicken-coop decor wasn't painful enough, the presentation of the farro summer salad was reminiscent of something served in a pig trough.'" As she read the rest, she pictured Nomi, sitting at her computer with an online thesaurus open on her screen, searching for synonyms to words like "disgusting" and "tasteless." In a couple hundred words, she had managed to work in "abominable," "noxious," and "odious."

While she felt immediate sympathy for the restaurant owners, the next emotion that hit was pity. Had Nomi initially been forced to write negative reviews as part of her job description? It seemed possible that a publication with the acronym *BAD* might gain followers because of their outrageous comments. But it also seemed probable that a person couldn't write such reviews unless she was already an angry person. What had put that massive chip on Nomi Fairchild's shoulder?

Debbie thought back to December, when interaction with former schoolteacher Rita Carson had revealed some things about the woman's life that had led her to becoming a bitter woman in her eighties. Now, months later, maybe no one would call her a sweet little old lady, but the change in her since townspeople had started visiting her and inviting her to functions was nothing short of remarkable. Maybe even what Nomi's granddaughters would call "a miracle." Could Paulette's "kill 'em with kindness" plan work on Nomi?

A few of Debbie's grandfather's sayings came to mind. "Can't make a silk purse out of a sow's ear," and "A leopard can't change its spots." To which Grandma was always quick to reply, "But with God, all things are possible."

Love your enemies. Pray for those who persecute you.

From the little contact she'd had already, she wasn't sure she had it in her to try too hard. But she'd experienced God's changes before— a heavenly infusion of compassion and patience that couldn't be explained in human terms.

As Ellie ushered Debbie and Janet into a small conference room at the library, she gestured to two stacks of papers and several books she'd arranged on the table in the middle of the room. "This was so fun. I found things about the Washburns and the Brittons. I got a little carried away and called the Northern Ohio Girl Scout office this morning. Hope I'm not overstepping my bounds. I don't want to steal any of the fun from you two."

"No apology needed," Debbie assured her. "We're grateful for any help."

"You have carte blanche to check out any leads you want." Janet pulled out a chair. "Can't wait to see what you came up with."

"Let me know if you think of anything else I can research. I wish I could stay in here with you, because I'd love to hear your reactions. But I'll be in and out."

Debbie set her laptop on the table then pulled a pen and note-book from her bag. "We'll keep a running list of what we learn." She took the chair next to Janet and drew a stack of papers toward her. The top papers were records documenting how Eric Britton had taken over the Washburn family construction business.

She flipped through a few more pages but didn't see Roxy's name anywhere. Then she pulled another stack toward her and found a black-and-white copy of a photograph. A woman who appeared to be in her late twenties or early thirties stood next to four teen girls, all dressed in shorts and short-sleeved blouses. The group stood in front of a small cabin.

The back of the photo had been copied on the same page. On it, a handwritten note said, *L to R: Troop #42 leader Francie Reese, Caroline Davis, Minnie Franklin, Roxy Britton, and Jade Tanaka. June 28, 1942, Camp Saundustee.*

The hair on Debbie's arms rose, and she angled the paper so Janet could see it too. Her friend whistled low. "Wow."

They now had full names and faces to go with them. She studied the figures. Francie, tall and willowy. Caroline, curvy with light blond hair. Minnie, with brown eyes and a pleasant face so much like Harry's. Roxy, her medium-dark hair curled under at her shoulders and pure mischief on her face. And lovely Jade...

Debbie rested a fingertip next to her. "What's her story?" she whispered. How did a Japanese girl end up in Ohio during World War II when so many Japanese people had been confined in camps?

"Now we know why they had to disguise her," Janet murmured with a bit of awe in her tone. "But what was she doing here in the first place?"

Debbie rested her hand on her stack of papers. "Hopefully we'll find some answers in all this, but let's do an internet search first."

"Good idea." Janet lifted her laptop out of a massive purse. "I'll take Caroline Davis and Minnie Franklin. We've already searched for Roxy, so you can have Francie and Jade."

"Sounds like a plan." Debbie opened her laptop. "I'm going to try finding an obituary for Francie. Kind of depressing, but it's unlikely she's still with us." She typed in *Francie Reese, Dennison, Ohio obituary*. In seconds, she found an entry from 2008.

FORMER GIRL SCOUT LEADER DIES AT 92
Francine "Francie" Elizabeth (née Jackson) Reese, 92, passed away at her home on October 4, 2008.

Debbie skimmed over the part about her education and her family, slowing when she reached the details that interested her.

Reese was affiliated with the Girl Scouts for forty years. For fifteen of those years, from 1947 to 1962, she served as the director of Camp Saundustee near Dennison, Ohio.

Below the funeral information were at least fifty comments. Debbie ran down the list, hunting for familiar names. She stopped when one jumped out at her.

Francie was not only a leader and mentor but also a dear friend. Her wisdom and compassion guided our troop, and her willingness to keep a confidence and leave her comfort zone quite literally saved lives. My lifelong friends and I are forever in her debt. You will be greatly missed, Francie.

The comment was signed. "Roxanne Keller." Debbie said the name out loud. "I think she's our Roxy." She read the comment to Janet.

"Saved lives?" Janet echoed. "What could a Girl Scout leader have done that would lead to saving lives?"

Debbie read the words again slowly. "'Her willingness to keep a confidence and leave her comfort zone,' apparently. Could it have something to do with Jade? They had to disguise her, so they didn't want somebody, maybe anybody, to realize she was Japanese. That might explain saving one life."

"Keep digging."

Debbie opened a new tab, and her fingers flew across the keys, typing in *Roxanne Keller, Dennison, Ohio*. Nothing. She tapped on the More Results button at the bottom of the page and was rewarded with a possibility. The article was from June of 2011.

Roxy B. Keller, author of more than twenty children's books, will be doing a reading and book signing on Saturday, July 9, from 1:00 to 3:00 at Chevalier's Books, Los Angeles's oldest indie bookstore, established in 1940.

Eighty-four-year-old Keller, known for her fictional tales of young, adventurous heroes inspired by real-life stories, will be reading from her latest chapter book for young adult readers, On My Own. *When asked how she manages to continue writing bestselling stories for teens in spite of the generation gap, Keller replied, "That gap is only there if we think it is. Kids today still experience the same trials my friends and I faced at their age. Wanting to be loved and accepted, feeling lonely and rejected at times, questioning our importance and our purpose—these are universal emotions that cross all generational boundaries."*

"I like her." Debbie hadn't meant to say it out loud. "Roxy was our kind of person."

"Was? She's gone?"

"I don't know yet. Checking that now." She put *Roxy B. Keller obituary* in the search space then closed her eyes for a moment. The young women in the picture were starting to become real. Had Debbie and Janet been born half a century earlier, they might have all been friends. It was a strange feeling, realizing she might be about to grieve someone she hadn't actually met.

She read the screen.

Acclaimed Author Roxy B. Keller Diagnosed with Cancer

She checked the date—five weeks ago. "Roxy might still be alive."

CHAPTER TEN

*D*ebbie padded barefoot into her kitchen on Tuesday evening, wearing capri pants and a sleeveless blouse. Her hair wasn't long enough for a stylish ponytail, but she'd put it up anyway. She was grateful that she didn't feel the need to be anything but comfortable with the people she'd invited for supper.

When Ashling had stopped in for her usual doughnut and coffee that morning, she'd appeared a bit frazzled, which was out of character for her. When Debbie asked her about it, the younger woman had admitted to feeling "a bit in over my head" with the Girl Scout informational meeting scheduled for tomorrow night and the overnight on Saturday.

So Debbie had invited her, Janet and Ian, and Greg and the boys over for a planning meeting for their "Star Party." Janet and Ian had a prior commitment, but Ashling and the Connors would be there. She also wanted to update them on what she and Janet had learned about Roxy and friends yesterday. She was taking hamburger seasonings out of the cupboard when her phone rang with a call from Harry.

"Hi, Harry. Did you get my message?"

"Sure did. Wish I could be more help. Minnie lives in Midvale with her niece. She had some kind of endoscopic procedure yesterday, so her voice was really hoarse. My hearing's not the best, and she has trouble speaking." He chuckled. "We make quite a pair. Anyway, she does want to talk to you when she can. I could tell she was interested in what you found in that old book. I gathered she'd never gone through it."

"I appreciate you calling her. Harry, do you remember hearing about a girl named Jade Tanaka in the forties?"

"Sounds like a name I might have heard, but no face comes to mind. Someone who lived here?"

"I think so. Minnie would have met her. Guess I'll have to wait and talk to her."

"I'm sure she'll be her usual chatty self in a day or two," Harry assured her. "I hope so, anyway. I'm as curious as you are now."

They hung up, and Debbie went back to dinner prep. As she shaped hamburger patties and seasoned them with salt, pepper, garlic powder, onion powder, and paprika, she listened to an audiobook of *On My Own* by Roxy B. Keller, hoping to find some hint of the author's own adventures as a teen.

As the second chapter began, she started to see some possible parallels. The heroine's name, for instance. A sixteen-year-old girl named Emmie, short for Emerald—a green gem, like Jade. But the story was set in northern California. The girl had been kidnapped and then escaped and was hiding in a redwood forest, living in a hollowed-out tree. Did the similarities end with the main character's name? How many horrible things had Jade been through?

Her thoughts were interrupted by the doorbell. "Come on in!" she called, as she washed her hands and grabbed a towel.

Julian walked into the kitchen first, carrying a paper bag filled with ears of sweet corn. "I found out something about your mystery."

Greg came in behind him. "Let's save it until everyone's here."

Julian nodded, but he appeared ready to burst with the restraint it took not to tell.

Next came Jaxon, alongside—to Debbie's surprise—a girl.

Slinging the towel over her shoulder, Debbie walked toward her and held out her hand. "I'm Debbie. Welcome."

The girl smiled shyly. "Nice to meet you. I'm Asuka. Jaxon told me about the book you found. I am very interested in what you discovered."

"Well, since you've already helped us solve part of the mystery, we would love to have you on our team."

"Jaxon showed me a picture of the flower you found. In Japan, monkshood is called *Yama-torikabuto*. It means 'bird's helmet.' I recognized it because my grandfather is a gardener. He always warned my brother and me never to touch it. I found out that as late as the 1870s, it was still being used by indigenous people in northern Japan called the Ainu. They hunted their sacred bears with poisoned arrow traps until the government prohibited it." The shy smile returned. "I am what you would call a history geek. I like learning of all kinds, and finding similarities between our cultures."

"Welcome to the club. I think everyone here is a bit of a history geek." Debbie pointed at Greg. "Especially him. Anything you want to know about American history, he can talk your ear off."

"Actually, I am hoping to learn about the girl who owned your book," Asuka answered. "I wonder why she was not in a detention camp. My grandfather has a friend who used to live in California, and he has collected many stories about Japanese Americans whose bank accounts were suddenly frozen, and they ended up in the camps. I wish I had paid more attention. Now I am interested in learning more about the life they were forced to live."

"It wasn't a proud moment in our history," Greg said, "but if we avoid talking about the truth of it, we're likely to forget the lessons we should have learned from it. I'd like to learn more about the camps myself."

The doorbell rang again, and Ashling came in. The conversation lightened as Jaxon introduced Asuka to Ashling.

When he mentioned Ashling was a Girl Scout leader, Asuka's countenance brightened. "At home, I am a Ranger scout. I think that would be a Senior here."

Ashling's eyes sparkled. "I'm brand-new at this. I'm leading Seniors, and I would absolutely love it if you'd join us while you're here. I know my girls would enjoy getting to know you, and it would be so fun to learn about scouting in another country."

"I told her about your Star Party," Jaxon said.

"That's great. I hope you can come. Maybe you could teach us some Japanese."

"I could teach the Girl Scout Promise." Asuka recited something in Japanese.

Ashling clapped her hands. "That would be perfect. Thank you."

"Right now," Greg said, "we're going to teach Asuka how to cook sweet corn the lazy man's way."

"Do you eat corn on the cob in Japan?" Ashling asked. "I apologize for my ignorance."

Jaxon grinned. "I asked her the same thing. Evidently the Japanese were eating corn long before the Pilgrims got here."

Asuka gave a small giggle. "No one needs to apologize. The whole point of exchange programs is so we can learn from each other. Yes, we eat corn on the cob and off it. We even put it on pizza."

Julian wrinkled his nose. "Really?"

"We should try it before we pass judgment," Debbie said. "I'm going to put the burgers on the grill. They won't take long."

Ashling held up the bowl she'd brought. "I'll mix the salad and add the croutons."

"I'll get started on the corn," Greg added.

"What do you need?" Debbie peeked into the bag. The corn hadn't been shucked yet. "I can get another paper bag for the husks, and I've got a canning kettle in the pantry that's—"

Greg stopped her with a hand. "All we need is a knife, a cutting board, and a microwave. No shucking involved."

"I think my father would like to learn this method," Asuka observed. "My mother and I do all the cooking, but she makes my father shuck the corn. I think my father would very much like an easier method."

Fifteen minutes later, Asuka laughed as she watched Greg shake a hot ear of corn out of its husk. His method involved cutting off one end and microwaving for three minutes. "We will never boil corn again," she said.

"I'm with you. This is so simple." Debbie handed a stack of plates to Jaxon and a handful of silverware to Julian. When Asuka held out her hand, she gave her the napkins. As she did, she asked, "Have you made any friends here yet?"

The shy but easy smile she'd witnessed in the past few minutes tightened. "Mr. and Mrs. Porter have been so kind to me."

That wasn't what she'd asked. She knew Mindy Porter, a teen who often came into the café with a group of friends. They apparently thrived on gossip and rumors. What would they do to this sweet girl? Though she'd only known Asuka for a few minutes, she couldn't imagine her joining in on such conversations.

She lowered her voice. "How are you and Mindy getting along?"

Asuka looked down at her feet. "We are not very much alike."

"Sometimes that happens," Debbie said. "I met two of the girls who are hoping to join Ashling's troop. I think you would get along well with them. You might be staying with the Porters, but that doesn't mean you and Mindy must have the same friends."

Asuka lifted her head, her smile back in place. "I am excited for the Star Party. I have been praying for the right friends here since I first filled out my application."

"I'll join you in that prayer."

"Thank you. Jaxon has been very kind as well. He's invited me to youth group, and I think I'll go. I miss my church."

"I belong to the same church he does, so I know most of those kids. They'll welcome you with open arms."

"I hope you are right." Her eyes glistened. "Could you do me the honor of calling me Suki? It is the name my family and close friends call me." She stared at her fingernails. "I was hesitant to ask anyone to call me that because it is a special name. But here, and with Jaxon's family, I feel welcome."

"I would be honored. And now, Suki, my friend, shall we eat?"

An enthusiastic nod answered her.

When they were all seated, Debbie offered a prayer, thanking God for each person at the table and asking His blessing on their planning. While everyone was busy dishing up and buttering corn, Greg nudged Julian with his elbow. "Okay. Now you can talk."

Julian let out a sigh that sounded like a balloon popping. "Finally." He grinned. "I went on a newspaper app and searched for murders in Dennison in the 1940s." His gaze swept the table, building suspense. "In June of 1942 a body was found in a shallow grave about five miles east of town. The authorities said the unidentified man died of 'unknown causes.' Get this. He was found five miles east of town, about a hundred yards off the tracks and right by the Girl Scout camp. I'm thinking the guy was poisoned—by Girl Scouts."

For several seconds, no one said a word. It struck Debbie that their immediate response at what should have been a preposterous theory was not laughter. "I want to say that's a crazy idea, Julian, but who knows? I do think we're getting closer to finding someone with answers, though." She told them about the picture of Roxy, Jade, and their friends, and about the article that mentioned Roxy's battle with cancer. "But I haven't found an obituary."

"If Roxy's still alive, we all need to go to California to meet her," Julian said.

Ashling laughed. "I like how you think." She turned to Debbie. "Did you try contacting her?"

"I sent a message through her author website. No telling how long it will take for her to get it, if she does at all. I imagine she has a secretary or assistant sorting through her correspondence. I mentioned Dennison in the first line of my message, hoping that would catch someone's attention."

"This is getting exciting," Ashling said.

"It is. I don't think I told any of you that Kim found out who donated the handbook. It was Harry's cousin, Minnie. She was one of the girls in the picture. She recently had a procedure that prevents her from talking much, but she should be able to share with us soon."

"Did you ask him about Jade?" Greg asked.

"Yes. He thought he might have heard her name, but couldn't remember anything. I'm anxious to talk to Minnie. She might be able to pull this all together for us."

The conversation moved on to plans for the Star Party. They talked about what everyone would need to bring and where they would hike on Sunday morning.

As they cleared the table, Ashling said, "Everyone is coming out to the camp around five thirty on Friday, but we have the cabins reserved starting at noon. So anyone who wants to go early can have a few hours to tromp around."

"Janet and I won't be able to get there until around four," Debbie said, "but we can divide and conquer from there. What's on the menu for supper?"

"Keeping it simple. I'll teach some fire-starting skills, and then we can roast hot dogs and heat baked beans. We'll do chips and veggies, and s'mores for dessert."

"I have never had a s'more," Suki said, her tone bright with excitement. "I suppose it sounds strange to all of you, but I have never been camping either."

"You won't be the only one," Ashling said. "There will be some twins with us who have never camped before either."

"I met Macy and Morgan," Debbie said. "They're the girls I told you about, Suki. I think you'll get along great with them." She turned to Ashling. "Which brings up another question. Do you have sleeping arrangements figured out?"

"I'm working on that." Ashling took a printed list out of a file folder. She slid it over to Debbie. "Maybe you can help me with it."

"I'd be happy to." The last word faded as a name jumped off the bottom of the sheet. Morgan and Macy were not coming alone.

Nomi Fairchild was coming to the Star Party.

Dennison, Ohio
May 31, 1942

Even though her two-block run was all downhill, Roxy was out of breath when she reached the corner and called Jade's name.

Jade spun toward her and beamed.

In seconds, Roxy was hugging her best friend in a tight embrace, almost knocking off her blond wig. "I'm so, so glad you're here." Her own eyes stung, but she knew they didn't have the luxury of a long, tearful reunion. She pulled away and grabbed one of Jade's suitcases. "Come with me. We can't be seen."

She'd had no time to come up with a plan and could only think of two options. They could go back up the hill and pray that Aunt Dolly and Emma May would hide Jade until dark, or they could show up at Francie's house unannounced with the same hope. "Follow me." She tugged on Jade's arm.

"If your mom doesn't want me here, I under—"

"It's not that. My mom's not here." She gave a brief explanation. "We have a safe place for you, but I can't get you there until I can sneak out after dark. My Girl Scout leader lives near here. You can stay with her until I can take you out there."

"Out where?"

"I'll explain everything, but right now we have to make sure no one sees you."

That was easier said than done on a beautiful Sunday morning when the whole town was walking home from church or working in gardens. Struggling with the heavy, awkward cases, they hurried through a parking lot, crossed a street, and cut through Francie's yard to get to her back door. Roxy had been hoping to find her in the garden. She didn't know Francie's new husband, James, well enough to have any idea what his reaction would be. Lord, keep us safe.

She knocked on the door, and Francie answered. Her hair was tied up in a scarf, and she wore a floral apron.

"Hi, Roxy. What a fun—" Her gaze landed on Jade, and she stepped back, swinging the door wide open.

"Is James home?" Roxy whispered. James, who was unfit for military service because of asthma, was one of the kindest men Roxy had ever met. And he was also a person who believed in doing the right thing. She couldn't be sure what that would mean in this situation.

"He's at his mother's all day," Francie said. "This must be Jade."

"Yes. And we need your help. Can you keep a secret?"

Francie bit her lip, appraising them in silence. Finally, she pointed to the kitchen table. The girls sat while she poured three glasses of lemonade then joined them at the table. "Start from the beginning."

Jade took a deep breath and began to tell her story. "My father is a pastor. He was born and raised in Japan. He moved to the States in 1924. For the past few years he has been translating the works of American preachers, like Charles Spurgeon and D. L. Moody, into Japanese and sending the manuscripts to our relatives in Japan, where they have been published. He was doing it all by hand until a few years ago when a wealthy man in our congregation bought him a Japanese typewriter. He taught me to use it, and I have been working with him."

"How wonderful," Francie murmured.

"When we were told we had to move, he was devastated. He was sure his typewriter would be confiscated. I could not bear to see him so heartbroken, so we made a hasty plan. We have heard that the government may soon be sending some people from the camps to work in the Midwest, so my parents may be able to join me here. My mother tried to call Roxy's. We didn't know she was in Washington, DC."

Roxy rested a hand on her friend's arm. "You did the right thing. You know Mom would have told you to come." She touched the tips of the platinum wig. "Where did you get this?"

A smile softened Jade's features. "A lady from our church works in the wardrobe department at MGM. She got me the wig and the giant sunglasses." The smile faded again. "I was so scared all the way here, but it was as if God had surrounded me with His angels. It's like a dream to finally be here."

"You're safe now." As she said the words, Roxy prayed they were true.

Francie tapped manicured fingers on the side of her glass. "But Caroline's father can't know she's here." Mr. Davis was not the only person in town with outspoken prejudices, but he might be the loudest.

"We have a place for her." Roxy told them both about the cabin. "But I need somewhere she'll be safe until about ten tonight when I can get out of the house."

Another long silence, and then a smile crinkled the skin around Francie's eyes. "I'm proud of you, Roxy. And yes, I'll help." She faced Jade. "You can stay here." She gestured toward a counter, where a sack of flour sat next to a white bowl and two bread pans. "You can help me bake bread, and then you can take a loaf with you. My husband will be home in a couple of hours, but you don't need to worry about him. Once he hears what you're doing, he'll probably offer to drive you to camp. Like Roxy said, you're safe here."

Roxy hoped Jade couldn't tell that Francie wasn't any more confident about those words than she had been.

CHAPTER ELEVEN

*D*ebbie walked through the depot's front door on Wednesday morning to find Kim putting the final touches on a display of eight-by-ten photos. They showed a sea of faces, more than a hundred former residents of Dennison.

Above the photos, she read the words NATIONAL PURPLE HEART DAY and the paragraph that followed.

> *National Purple Heart Day, established in 2014, is observed on August 7 each year. It is a day of remembrance for our nation to honor those who were wounded or who sacrificed their lives on the battlefield.*

Debbie scanned the photographs, recognizing names and faces. Ray Zink, the man she'd bought her house from, wounded in World War II. Greg's grandfather, who had never returned from the same war. A man her father had gone to high school with who was killed in Vietnam.

She thought of the stories she'd collected from interviews with Dennison's Greatest Generation, including Kim's mother, Eileen Palmer, who'd stepped up at the young age of twenty to take over the job of stationmaster at the depot. Thousands of soldiers had stopped at this depot on their way to war. Romances, friendships, and decades of correspondence had begun right here in this building. And many who had left from this depot had paid the ultimate price.

"Thank you for doing this," Debbie said.

"They deserve it," Kim answered. "We owe them everything."

After another moment of silence, Debbie took a deep breath and shifted her mind to the things at hand. When she walked into the café, she pulled a red, white, and blue apron covered with stars and stripes from the apron drawer.

She greeted Janet then laughed at the words on her T-shirt— ROLLIN' IN THE DOUGH. "Don't you wish."

"Hey, I'd take this job over big bucks any day, wouldn't you?"

"Yes, I would." It wasn't all that long ago that she'd questioned whether leaving her job in Cleveland had been the right decision. But now, even on their busiest days, even when the fryer broke or the pastry case emptied before noon, even when they got their first one-star review, she wouldn't trade this place for the stress of the corporate job she'd left behind. "I'd do it all over again in a heart-beat." While she was thinking about one-star reviews, she added, "Nomi Fairchild is coming to the Star Party."

Janet fumbled a tray of doughnuts and nearly sent them top-pling to the floor. "Why?"

"Evidently she's chaperoning her granddaughters."

"But I heard her grumbling when one of the girls said they hoped they could go."

Debbie nodded, recalling Nomi's exact words when Morgan said they'd never done anything like camping. *For good reason. Like snakes and mosquitos and smoke.*

Janet opened the pastry case and slid the tray of doughnuts into place. "Love your enemies. Pray for those who persecute you. We'll get through this."

"Finally." Debbie sat at her kitchen table and aimed the words at the box labeled GIRL SCOUTS WWII. The box she had wanted to get to since finding it in the depot storeroom five days earlier. While she didn't have high hopes of finding anything directly relating to Jade, she'd been excited to get a bigger picture of what scouting had been like during the war.

She took the lid off the box, and then her phone dinged with a text message. Greg.

Her lips curved up at the sight of his name. Her smile widened as she read the first line.

TWO THINGS. FIRST: SUKI ASKED JAXON TO ASK YOU FOR WHATEVER INFORMATION YOU CAN GIVE HER ABOUT JADE. SHE WANTS TO TALK TO HER GRANDFATHER AND SEE IF HE CAN FIND OUT ANYTHING ABOUT HER FAMILY.

Suki's phone number followed. Debbie answered with, DEFINITELY, AND THANK YOU. And then her smile faded. Her heart sank as she read Greg's next message.

SORRY TO KEEP ASKING "DID YOU SEE THIS?" BUT DID YOU? THIS ONE COULD BE CONSTRUED AS BETTER, I GUESS. HOPE IT GENERATES THE SAME PUSHBACK AS THE LAST ONE, THOUGH I SUPPOSE WITH ARTICLES LIKE THESE, THEY DON'T CARE IF THE RESPONSE IS POSITIVE OR NEGATIVE, AS LONG AS IT'S BIG.

Below that dire line was a link to the Gastro Gnome blog. She opened it and stared at the heading: TRIED AGAIN. STILL NOT IMPRESSED. Holding her breath, she continued to read.

> *Like most grandmothers, I'll do nearly anything to make my granddaughters happy. But when they asked to have breakfast at the Whistle Stop Café in Dennison, Ohio, I almost said no. If you've been following, you know I tried it last week and the wait was so long I nearly left.*
>
> *Because I'm a softy when it comes to my girls, I relented. I will say, we were ushered to a table quickly—likely out of fear of another honest review—but from there on, my reaction was tepid at best. The acoustics in the place are awful. The high ceilings and wood floors don't allow for sound absorption...*

Debbie stopped reading when she realized the fingers on her right hand were curling into a fist. She skimmed the rest, gritting her teeth over phrases like, "Omelet was adequate," "Coffee is tolerable," and "The girls, at least, managed to enjoy their pancakes."

She wanted to spew a few well-chosen phrases herself, but she took several deep breaths and repeated what was now becoming her motto. "Love your enemies. Pray for those who persecute you. We'll get through this."

She responded to Greg's text with an angry emoji and the words. THE GNOME IS COMING TO THE STAR PARTY. ASKING THE LORD TO TOUGHEN MY SKIN AND SOFTEN MY HEART BEFORE SATURDAY NIGHT.

Then she refocused her attention on the box.

The first things she pulled out were three tattered three-ring notebooks. A piece of once-white tape was stuck to the front of the first one, with smudged blue words spelling out *Minutes – Troop 42*.

Roxy's troop. With careful movements, she set the book on the table and opened to the first page. Neat cursive writing filled it.

> *September 9, 1931*
> *This is the first meeting of the Junior and Senior Girl Scout Troop 42. The meeting began with a prayer by our leader, Mrs. Olsten, followed by the Pledge of Allegiance, and the Girl Scout Promise and Pledge. Next, we all introduced ourselves and then held an election of officers.*

The entry was written when Roxy had been about six, but Debbie ran down the short list of names anyway, searching for anything familiar. She smiled when she spotted a name she recognized.

Francine Jackson, Secretary

Francie, who later became Francie Reese, the first director of Camp Saundustee. Francie would have been in her midteens at the time, since she was about ten years older than Roxy.

Debbie paged through, smiling at the things these girls planned that most of the teens she knew today wouldn't even think of. Things like "Learned flag signals today. We will start working on Morse Code at our next meeting," and "Mr. Olsten is helping us make our own birchbark canoe."

The last entry in that book was in May of 1933. She closed it then checked the dates of the others. The last one began on August 25, 1941. She glanced at the list of scouts in attendance at the first meeting and found the names she was hoping for. Roxy Britton, Caroline Davis, Minnie Franklin, and their leader, Francie Reese.

Debbie carried the book and her glass of ice water into the living room. On her way, she glanced at the time on the microwave. She had a full hour until she needed to get ready for the scout meeting at the high school.

She skimmed each page, fascinated by the activities Francie listed. Daylong hikes, making paper flowers, planting moss gardens, and baking cookies for shut-ins. Her troop had learned about knot tying, play production, milk pasteurization, Morse code, citizenship, vegetable dyes, rock identification, and how to make a signal fire. Ashling would love this.

But when Debbie got to January of 1942, the tone changed. Fewer fun activities and less emphasis on learning new skills. The minutes were filled with plans for newspaper and scrap metal drives, offering childcare for working mothers whose husbands were deployed, planting victory gardens, and volunteering at the depot. One entry read:

> *Our families have been saving sugar for two months so we could bake cookies for the soldiers for Easter. On Friday after school, some of us—Caroline, Betty, Madeline, Minnie, Diana, Connie, and Roxy—met at Francie's house to bake for the Salvation Army. We made six dozen oatmeal raisin and*

five dozen molasses cookies. On Saturday, we handed them out. We all hope we were able to bring a little happiness to the soldiers who are away from their families on this holiday.

Though she wasn't cooking for soldiers on active duty, Debbie had waited on several veterans this morning. Ray Zink had come in with his sister, Gayle, who was visiting from Columbus. They'd been with Madeline O'Sullivan, Carly O'Sullivan's ninety-four-year-old grandmother, who was very likely the Madeline in the list of the girls who'd made Easter cookies for soldiers.

Debbie did the math. Madeline would have been about twelve when this entry was written.

Would Madeline remember anything about Roxy, Caroline, Minnie, or maybe even Jade?

She picked up her phone and found Madeline's number. As it rang, she pictured Madeline, always fashionably dressed, sitting regally in one of the wingback chairs in a cozy alcove in her apartment at Good Shepherd Retirement Center. Her silvery hair would be perfectly coiffed, kept in the latest style by Carly, who owned Serenity Salon & Spa on Main Street.

Debbie got up and paced as she waited, feeling strangely jittery with the anticipation of possibly getting some answers.

Finally, Madeline's sweet voice came down the line. "Good afternoon, Debbie. How are you?"

"I'm doing great. Do you have a few minutes to talk?"

Madeline's laughter drifted through the phone, light and airy. "Time is something we all have here, for as long as the Lord grants it. What can I do for you, dear? More history questions?"

"Yes," Debbie admitted sheepishly. "I hope my questions never get annoying."

"Not at all. I hope it didn't sound like I was complaining. I love reminiscing and sharing stories, and you always appreciate the interesting ones."

"That's very gracious of you. I'm wondering what you can tell me about a couple of the girls in Girl Scouts with you in 1942."

"I will give it my best shot. There are a few of us still breathing, so if I can't give you what you need, we might be able to find someone who can."

"The girls I'm wondering about are Roxy Britton and Caroline Davis. Minnie Franklin is another one, but I have a way to get in touch with her."

"I was friends with Roxy's sister, Diana. Did you know Roxy became an author?"

"I've started listening to an audio version of one of her books. I found a Girl Scout handbook that used to be hers, and I'd love to talk to her if she's still able. I sent a message through her website, but I'm not sure she'll get it. I read that she has cancer. Are you still in contact with her or her sister?"

"Their family moved back to California sometime in the forties, but I still hear from Diana at Christmas. She always writes a newsy letter."

Debbie hesitated then opted for one of her father's favorite expressions. Nothing ventured, nothing gained. "Would you be willing to share her address?"

"I can do you one better. I have Diana's phone number. Last I heard, Roxy was in a facility a block from her house. Diana won't answer if she doesn't recognize the number, but if you'd like to come here sometime, we could call her together."

Debbie's felt her pulse pick up. "That would be fantastic. Another question. Do you remember a girl named Jade?"

"Now there's a name I haven't heard in forever. Jade Tanaka. Really sweet lady. She lived in California. I think she and Roxy had been friends since they were babies."

Sweet *lady*? So Jade might have stayed in Dennison into adulthood or at least returned to visit. "What do you remember about Jade when she was here during World War II?"

"Here? Not sure where you heard that, but she definitely wasn't here during the war. I remember Roxy asking us all to pray for the Tanaka family because they were confined in a camp. In Arizona, I think."

Debbie walked into the living room and stared down at the picture taken at Camp Saundustee in June of 1942. "You're sure she was never here? Maybe in 1942?"

"I'm sure. I met Jade when she came to Dennison with Roxy sometime in the fifties. I would have remembered if she was here during the war. A Japanese girl in town after Pearl Harbor would have caused a huge stir. For her sake, the Brittons would never have allowed that."

And yet Debbie had seen the photo and the secretive references to Jade's presence in town. How could that be?

Madeline continued. "In fact, now that I think about it, Roxy and Diana's parents might not have even been here in 1942. Their mother was a nurse, stationed somewhere for a while, and her father was serving overseas. The girls lived with Caroline Davis's family during that time. But even if the Brittons were here, they wouldn't have put Jade or themselves at risk like that. Considering the strong prejudices at the time, at the very least, they would have been harassed."

Debbie finished the call more confused than she had been before it. Somehow, the more she learned, the less was clear about Jade Tanaka.

CHAPTER TWELVE

anet arranged platters of trefoil-shaped green-frosted sugar cookies she'd made from the original Girl Scout cookie recipe Debbie had found online. Debbie moved a table so it faced the door of the high school cafeteria. On it, she set markers, name tags, and the information sheets Ashling had made to explain the hands-on part of the meeting.

Ashling had thought it would be helpful to introduce the girls to some of the activities they'd participate in if they joined her troop. They'd arranged six tables, each labeled with signs describing a craft or skill to be learned. After the informational part of the meeting, the girls would take turns visiting the different tables and experiencing Girl Scout activities. Debbie would be stationed at a table already supplied with index cards. As she had volunteered to do for a couple of meetings throughout the year, she would be introducing the girls to tips for recording family stories and learning more about their heritage.

A few minutes after six, Ashling walked up to the table. Her stress level was evident in the strain on her face and tension in her shoulders.

"What's wrong?" Debbie asked her.

Ashling clenched her hands into fists. "What if no one shows?"

"That's not going to happen. You know that." Debbie glanced at the clock. A quarter after six was still early. Resting her hand on Ashling's shoulder, she offered up a short prayer, asking that Ashling's fear wouldn't be realized, and that, no matter how many people showed up, the evening would be considered a success by everyone in attendance.

At 6:17, her prayer was answered as two giggling girls walked through the doors, followed by two sets of parents.

The third girl to walk through the door was Suki, accompanied by Kathleen Porter, Mindy's mom. Mindy herself was nowhere to be seen. Debbie was the closest to the door, so she greeted them, giving Suki a hug then directing them to fill out name tags. "If you want, draw something on your tag that says something about you." She watched as Suki wrote *Asuka* in English then artfully added a Japanese character.

"What does it mean?" Debbie asked.

"It is the symbol for bird. There are a couple of possible origins for my name, but I prefer the one that means 'flying bird.'"

"Well, you and I can fly around together. My name means 'bee.' And I will pray that you soar while you are here, flying bird."

As Suki and Kathleen picked up some of the information on the table, Debbie watched the door. She hoped some of the girls she knew from church would arrive soon so she could introduce them to Suki.

The next arrivals warmed her heart, right before her blood ran cold. Macy and Morgan. Followed by their grandmother.

Debbie steadied her breath and repeated her go-to words, followed by the next line from the twelfth chapter of Romans. *Bless those who persecute you; bless and do not curse them.*

Where were the twins' parents? After greeting the girls with a warm smile, she welcomed Nomi with all the heartfelt warmth she could muster then motioned for Suki to join them and made introductions.

Suki explained the handouts to Morgan and Macy and told them about adding a picture to their name tags. Without any verbal conversation, Morgan drew the right half of a heart and Macy drew the left half on hers.

Judging by the laughter and chatter that followed, Suki was going to be fine. Debbie turned to Nomi and thought of another part of Romans 12. *If your enemy is hungry, feed him.* Or her, as the case may be. To be fair, they had tried to feed her multiple times and failed to soften her heart, but it seemed to be the best way of winning over Gastro Gnome. With a brighter smile than she felt like giving, Debbie invited Nomi to follow her to the coffee and cookies.

Distrust crossed the critic's face. What was she thinking?

"Janet used the original Girl Scout cookie recipe," Debbie explained. No matter what this woman said about her and her business, she was determined to stay on the high road.

As Nomi took a small paper plate and reached for a cookie, Janet locked eyes with Debbie. Her expression was more readable. She was incredibly nervous, and Debbie understood why. This woman's poison pen could do them much harm.

To her surprise, Nomi took a bite and merely nodded. Was it a nod of approval? Since she took a cup of coffee and moved away to find a seat, they might never know. Debbie shrugged. "Could have been worse."

"Much worse." Janet copied the rise and fall of Debbie's shoulders. "Got to shrug it off, right?"

"Right." Debbie's gaze followed Nomi as she sat at the end of a row, lifted the coffee to her lips, and grimaced.

Janet laughed. "Well then. At least I can tell what she means by that."

Debbie returned to her post by the cafeteria door and was overjoyed to see a line at the registration table. Within minutes, most of the chairs were filled. Eleven girls had signed in. Four were already part of the troop Ashling led. Eleven was a good number. Ashling would be thrilled.

Greg was the last person to walk in, lugging a telescope and several thick books. "Sorry I'm late," he whispered, coming up beside her and giving her a quick one-armed hug.

"No worries." If he'd done something that actually required an apology, she'd likely have the same reaction. His smile always made her melt.

Ashling started the meeting by giving a brief history of the Girl Scouts. Her thick copper braid swayed as she went through a short presentation. "Our founder, Juliette Gordon Low, who also went by 'Daisy,' started Girl Scouts in 1912 in her hometown of Savannah, Georgia. The first troop was made up of eighteen girls."

Debbie remembered this from her own years in Girl Scouts, and she enjoyed revisiting it.

"Back then, women didn't yet have the right to vote. Daisy's ideas for helping girls develop their unique strengths was revolutionary. The opportunities she provided have had a ripple effect that is still helping girls discover their full potential and make lasting friendships today."

Next, she showed a series of historical photographs. One was a picture of Mrs. Sarah Randolph Bailey, who played an important role in the desegregation of the Girl Scouts and was awarded the group's highest honor, the Thanks Badge. Another pictured several members of Troop 42 volunteering at the depot Salvation Army canteen in 1942. The shot included Roxy and Caroline.

From there, she talked about the plans she had for the year, including the Star Party and her intent to call on the expertise of many Dennison residents. Then she introduced the activity tables. When she opened the meeting up for questions, one woman asked if Ashling needed more volunteers, saying she'd love to teach quilting if the girls were interested.

The next hand to shoot in the air sported a ring on each finger. Debbie wasn't sure if Ashling knew anything about the café's encounters with Nomi, and hoped they'd see a kinder, gentler side of her here.

"How old are you, Miss Kelly?" Nomi's tone was the same as the one she'd used to "suggest" hollandaise sauce. *Accusatory* was the word that came to Debbie's mind.

"I'm twenty." Ashling's infectious smile should have inspired confidence, but Debbie had a feeling the number of years she'd lived—or rather, the number of years she hadn't—would cancel that out in Nomi's captious mind.

Indeed, she seemed about to speak, but Ashling was prepared for that question. "I am fully aware that I haven't had much more life experience than many of the girls I'll be leading, which is why I've enlisted the help of some amazing volunteers. Let me introduce the ones who are in attendance. Such as Ian Shaw, the chief of our police department, who has graciously volunteered to talk to us about community safety and careers in law enforcement."

Ian, with his secure stance and captivating brogue, stood and sang Ashling's praises. "My wife and I have known Ashling Kelly since she was a little girl. She has spent countless hours with our family, and we've hired her on more than one occasion to do repair jobs that were far beyond my abilities. One of the things I admire most about her is that she's never been afraid to ask for help. We're proud of her and happy to lend a hand, the same way she never hesitates to."

By the time Ashling had presented the president of the chamber of commerce, the head librarian of the public library, a registered nurse, an art teacher, the director of the depot museum, and the owners of the Whistle Stop Café, a bit of the stiffness seemed to have seeped from Nomi's posture.

For the last hour, the girls and any parents who were interested rotated from table to table, exploring the various activities.

Debbie would introduce herself and then explain, "In the past year I've recorded stories of some of our town's oldest citizens. I'm so excited that we now have audio and video recordings of stories going back more than a hundred years. Some of our oldest residents shared their ancestors' stories from as far back as the Civil War. This rich history could have been lost. I'm sure many of you have grandparents, aunts, uncles, or neighbors who would love to share 'tales of long ago,' legacies that you may someday pass on to your grandchildren."

She usually got several smiles and nods at that point.

"If preserving stories from older generations is something that interests you, I'll be sharing tips on how to go about it. We'll talk about how to create a family tree and how to find information about your ancestors. We'll create a family history game, talk about and prepare traditional foods in your family, and may even create photo albums with pictures of homes where your ancestors lived and heirloom keepsakes your family may have collected over the years. And we'll learn how to conduct interviews. Here are a few sample questions." She handed each person a sheet of paper.

Where did you grow up?
What were your parents like? Your siblings?
What do you remember about your grandparents?
Who were your friends?
What was school like for you?
What did you do for fun when you were a child?
   When you were a teenager?
What movies and songs did you like when you were young?
How did you meet your spouse?
What important lessons have you learned in your life?

Debbie finished with, "Can any of you pick one of these questions and answer it as if you were your parent or someone from an earlier generation?"

By the time the next-to-the-last group left her table, she'd learned things she'd never heard about several Dennison families, going back over a century. And now, Macy, Morgan, and Suki sat in front of her as she asked them to answer a question as one of their ancestors.

Morgan raised her hand. "I can answer one. It's kind of sad." Her voice lowered. "My name is Nomi Fairchild. When I was born, my left eye turned in. Today they would call it lazy eye. My parents couldn't afford the surgery to fix it, so all through elementary school I was teased unmercifully. I was called 'Cross Eye.' Only my teachers used my real name. I didn't have any friends."

Debbie had wondered if Nomi's hard exterior had been caused by something in her youth, but the actual story struck Debbie to the core.

"When I was fifteen, I was shocked when a boy asked me to a dance," Morgan continued. "I bought a new dress, and I was so excited—but he stood me up. That's when I found out he'd won a bet by asking me out. That's when I dropped out of school and moved to New York. I lived in a homeless shelter until I got a job in a restaurant and could afford my own place. Then I put myself through night school and worked sixty hours a week until I finally got a job with insurance that would cover my surgery."

Debbie swallowed against the tightness in her throat.

"After my eyes were fixed, I made a lot of friends. But I didn't trust any of them. If people can't look beyond what's on the outside, they aren't really friends."

Debbie sat in silence for a moment, then glanced to her right, where Nomi sat alone in a folding chair, tapping on her phone. "I'm sure that kind of hurt affected her whole life."

Macy nodded. "Please don't let her know we told you. She really is a good person inside."

"I won't say anything. Would you mind if I share that with Janet?"

Morgan shook her head. "I think it helps people understand why she is the way she is. We're sorry about the reviews she gave you. The café is awesome."

"Thank you for telling me," Debbie said to the twins. "Your secret is safe with me." At last, she finally felt as if she could begin to understand Gastro Gnome.

Dennison, Ohio
June 1, 1942

Roxy was hot, sweaty, and out of breath by the time she reached the little cabin early Monday afternoon. When she hopped off her bike, she could feel her heart pounding. Partly from exertion, partly from fear.

Was Jade okay? How had she handled her first night alone? Was she scared or lonely? Had the night sounds in the woods rather than a big city scared her? Did she resent having to hide way out here, all alone? Would she be mad at Roxy? But what other choices did she have?

Trying to still her mind, Roxy leaned her bicycle against the cabin, then stopped and sniffed the air. What was that smell?

Food. Her chest tightened. *They'd left Jade with a loaf of bread, a tin of butter, and a jar of peanut butter. Was someone else here?* The air seeped from her lungs. *There, a few yards behind the cabin, was a ring of rocks. A bit of smoke drifted up from what was left of a campfire. A stick with one end whittled to a sharp point rested against the rocks.*

She climbed the cabin steps and knocked out the Morse code they'd agreed on. R *for Roxy. Though the precaution seemed silly now that she realized Jade had announced her presence with smoke from the fire. She took a calming breath. She was being paranoid. No one was watching.*

The door swung open, and a smiling Jade stood in front of her, barefoot in shorts and a sleeveless blouse. "Good morning. Welcome to my home." She stepped back and made a sweeping gesture to invite Roxy in.

"You made a fire." She didn't hide the surprise in her voice.

"Yep. I had peanut butter toast for breakfast."

"You're incredible. How does a girl from Los Angeles know how to build a campfire?"

Jade laughed. "Girl Scouts."

"Well, you probably don't need this then." Roxy pulled her Girl Scout handbook out of her haversack.

"I thought it might have some outdoor skills you could use, but it sounds like you know it all already." She handed her the book and Jade hugged her.

Roxy jumped back. "Why is your hair wet?"

"I took a shower."

"You what?" Roxy eyed the two brown glass jugs of water James had set on the floor. They were still in the corner where he'd left them. One was a third empty. Not enough for hair washing.

"There's a waterfall nearby. Have you seen it? I have my own waterfall right in my backyard."

"I had no idea. Are you all right? Was it scary out here last night?" Roxy's gaze took in the room. A chipped blue-glass canning jar sat on the little table, filled with purple lilacs. She slid her arms out of her haversack and let it fall to the floor. It landed next to a weathered wooden crate that held a bouquet of daisies in a rusted coffee can. "I like what you've done to the place."

"I woke up early and had to go exploring. This place is like heaven. I found a spring. Water bubbling right up from the ground and as clean as it can be. I can fill the bottles from that, so you won't have to bring me water. In a couple of weeks I'll have wild strawberries, and I found raspberry bushes. This must be what the

Garden of Eden felt like. Come on. I'll show you." She slid her feet into sandals, giving Roxy a minute to process the happy chatter.

"So you're not upset about being way out here?"

"Upset?" Jade gaped at her like she'd said something preposterous. "Never in my wildest dreams could I have imagined a more perfect place to work. And live. To be honest, I was afraid that if I was staying with you and your mom, life would be too busy for me to get any translating done, or I'd be constantly worrying about what people thought of you or might do to you because of how they felt about me. This is perfect." She opened the door and repeated the same hand sweep. "First, the waterfall, then—"

A loud crash halted her words. Wide-eyed, she stared at Roxy.

Roxy held her breath. She and Caroline and Minnie had walked all around the perimeter of the camp on Friday afternoon. They hadn't seen or heard any evidence that anyone had been on the property recently. She closed her eyes and strained her ears. Silence.

"Probably a tree falling," she said, her voice low, proving she wasn't confident in her assumption.

"There's no wind."

"Maybe it was rotten. Dead trees fall all the time, don't they?" Roxy gave the most convincing smile she could manage. "Come on. Show me your waterfall."

As Jade led her toward the path, Roxy bent and scooped up a dead branch.

Just in case.

CHAPTER THIRTEEN

S o they hid her." On Thursday afternoon, Janet set two glasses of iced tea on a table by the front windows at the café and took a chair across from Debbie.

"That's my guess." It had been another busy day. This was the first chance she'd had to tell Janet what she'd learned from Madeline. "Madeline was friends with Roxy's little sister. If Jade had been living with Roxy's family, she would have known."

"But the scout leader and two of Roxy's friends knew. Were they the only ones? And why take the chance of a photo if they were trying to keep her a secret?"

Debbie held up her index finger. "I discovered something about that photo." She pulled her phone out of her apron pocket and accessed the picture she'd taken of the photograph. "The date stamped on the border."

Janet's lips parted. "May 12, 1948." Her eyes widened. "That's six years after the time Jade was here. So they kept the film and didn't have it developed until it was safe?"

"I think so, yeah."

"How do you hide a teenager? And was she here alone or with her family?" Janet's expression said she was probably imagining her own family in a similar situation.

"Maybe they sent her here to protect her. Or maybe she was in a camp and escaped. I read somewhere that the penalty for refusing to go to a detention camp was ninety days in prison. I have no idea what they would have done to a minor if she was caught. And Madeline was convinced it wouldn't have been safe for Jade to be here." She pointed to her phone. "That picture was taken at Camp Saundustee. The camp didn't open until after the war, but—"

"Some of the construction had already been done." Janet finished her sentence, as she'd been doing for thirty years.

"She could have hidden in one of the buildings. Maybe the cabin they're standing in front of in the picture. That would explain Jade's Shower. Maybe it was literally the place where she took showers."

Janet clicked her fingernails on the side of her glass. "I know kids were used to more freedom back then. The world was a scarier place in some ways, but here in the Midwest, people didn't talk about stranger danger like we do today. So I may sound like an overprotective modern mom, but I can't imagine Roxy's parents sticking the poor girl out in the wilderness all by herself. Think of all we've read about people in Europe hiding Jewish people. Or stations on the Underground Railroad. They usually used attics and cellars and barns near where they lived. Saundustee is five miles outside of town. Wouldn't it have been smarter to hide her in their attic?"

"You read *The Diary of Anne Frank*. Being a teenage girl and having to be shut up in an attic or basement, maybe for the duration of the war, never allowed to go outside—it would have been miserable. Imagine having a two-hundred-and-fifty-acre park to roam around in instead."

Janet scrunched her mouth to one side. "I get that. But no electricity or running water?" She sighed. "I suppose I'm thinking like a fortysomething. If I imagine Tiffany or Ashling at that age, given the choice of being cooped up in an attic or allowed to run free in nature, I know what they'd choose."

Debbie reached for her phone. "I'm going to call Madeline and see if we can arrange a phone call with Roxy's sister." She put the call on speakerphone.

"Hi, Debbie." Madeline's voice sounded flat. "I was about to call you."

"Is everything all right?"

Madeline's sigh was audible. "After speaking with you yesterday, I decided to be proactive and give Diana a call. I left a message, and she returned my call a few minutes ago. I wish I had better news. They've had to put Roxy on hospice care."

Debbie stared at the swirl of cream in her coffee cup. After talking to Madeline, she'd felt the need for something warm to ease the chill that had settled inside her in spite of the heat. "It's so sad. Selfishly, I'm thinking of all we might have learned from her if I'd searched for that book a week earlier."

"God knew." Janet stirred sugar into the coffee Debbie had brought her. "The timing isn't an accident."

It might not make sense right now, but God's timing was always perfect. "Change of subject. I learned something about Nomi last night." She shared what the girls had given her permission to tell Janet.

"That explains so much. And with the latest rejection, being sued and losing her job—I actually feel sorry for her."

"Hurt people hurt people," Debbie said. "Sounds like she's spent her whole life as a porcupine, trying to protect herself by attacking others."

"Reminds me of Rita Carson."

Debbie took a sip of coffee. "I had the same thought. And look at her now."

"Once she cracked out of that ugly cocoon, we saw her true, beautiful colors."

Debbie laughed. "Porcupines and butterflies. We're really mixing our metaphors, but it all comes out the same way. That there's hope for Nomi." They sat in comfortable silence for several minutes until a buzz from Debbie's phone interrupted the stillness.

"Don't keep the man waiting." Janet picked up her mug and stood. "See you in the morning."

She answered the phone with a small smile.

"Hey, how was your day?" Greg asked.

"Busy, but good. Yours?"

"Hot, but good. We were short a couple guys, so I ended up helping roofers. I'm getting too old for that kind of work, but we're supposed to get rain in the next couple of days, so we had to get it done. Anyway, we knocked off early. I'm showered and cooled off. Trying to figure out what to feed the bottomless boys. And a girl."

"Girl? Do tell."

"That's why I called. Or at least I'll claim that as my excuse this time. Suki's here. Her grandfather's friend found some information on the Tanakas."

"That was quick."

"It sounds like he's spent decades researching people who were confined. Besides publishing their stories, he's compiled an extensive database of thousands of families."

"I can't wait to see what he's found."

"If you're free, we could drop over."

"I'm still at work, but I'll be home in a few minutes. How about I order pizza?"

"You've been feeding us a lot lately."

"I enjoy it." *And it's something I hope to do a lot more in the not-too-distant future.*

"Sounds fun. But I owe you. How about I take you out on Saturday night? Picture it—you, me, a star-filled sky and a crackling fire…"

She laughed. "You, me, and twenty other people. Sounds cozy."

"Doesn't it? I'll make you the perfect s'more then serenade you with peaceful campfire songs."

Debbie laughed. "Not sure how peaceful that would end up. I seem to recall a chilly picnic with you and your boys in December in which a heated argument broke out over how to toast the perfect marshmallow. Besides, we should sing classic Girl Scout campfire songs to stay on theme."

"You sure know how to kill a romantic evening."

"That's okay. You'll make it up to me."

"Yes, I will." The smile in his voice warmed her to her toes. "What time should we come?"

"How about five? Think Buona Vita will make corn pizza for us?"

"Worth a shot, I guess."

"Maybe we'll start a new trend."

Greg laughed. "See you at five."

And there went her evening of going through the rest of the things in the Girl Scout box. But it would be much more fun with a group. She stopped Janet, who had her purse slung over her shoulder and her hand on the door handle. "Any extra dessert goodies in the freezer?"

Janet smiled knowingly. "Entertaining someone tonight?"

"A few someones, in fact. And you're welcome to join us. Suki found out something about Jade's parents."

"Aw, I can't. Mom and Dad are coming for dinner."

"I'll tell you everything tomorrow. What about that dessert?"

Janet propped one hand on her hip and tilted her head. "Does a one-legged duck swim in a circle?"

Debbie rolled her eyes. They'd heard Harry use that one more than once. "Thank you."

"Anytime." Janet nodded toward the kitchen. "There are some oatmeal raisin cookies, part of a carrot cake, and a few dozen dough-nuts bagged in half dozens."

"You're amazing."

"Don't you forget it." With a wink, Janet opened the door and waved.

Debbie took two packages of doughnuts out of the freezer, closed the door, and then gave in to second thoughts and took out another package. She'd seen the boys scarf down doughnuts.

By the time she got home, it was almost four. She showered and changed into shorts and a T-shirt. She did a search for Japanese pizza toppings. Did they put the corn on raw? What she found was interesting. Corn was indeed a popular topping. So was tuna fish, among other seafood items.

She made the call to Buona Vita. The boy who answered the phone was a frequent café customer and friend of Jaxon's. He sounded confused when she asked if corn was a possible topping. So she educated him on what she'd learned about pizza toppings in Japan. When she told him about the recipe she'd found for tuna and corn pizza, she was afraid he might gag.

"Should I plan to add it myself?" she asked.

"This time, but let me know what you think about it. Maybe I'll get the manager to add corn to our options. But it's a big no on the tuna."

"I have to agree."

With everything ready for her second night of hospitality in three days, she put on water to boil for another pot of strong traditional tea then cut corn kernels off the three cobs left over from Tuesday night. Already cooked, it would be easy to sauté the kernels until they were slightly caramelized.

And then she sat at the table with the contents of the box. She stacked the Troop 42 meeting minutes notebooks on her left then reached in for the next item. Another notebook. This one had a brown cover that wrapped around the whole book and was secured with a strip of leather. The leather crackled a bit as she unwound the tie and opened it.

Goose bumps rose on her arms when she saw the name inside the cover. *Francie Reese.* Scout leader for Troop 42. The woman who had become the first director of Camp Saundustee. She turned several pages. It wasn't exactly a journal. It appeared to be a mixture of brainstorming ideas, supply lists, doodles, and notes about some of the troop activities. The pages weren't always dated, but there were occasional dates throughout, though no years. She leafed through, hoping to find something that might give a hint at Francie's involvement with Jade. She was, after all, in the photograph.

There were pages covered with nothing but doodling. Francie had possessed some artistic talent. An apple, a lit candle, a pine tree, a log cabin. Debbie smiled, thinking how often she'd done the same while listening to a lecture in college or trying to stay awake during a boring business meeting.

Over halfway through the notebook, she found a to-do list. Under *Sweep porch* and *4 loaves* were the words, *Bread, cheese, & fruit to J.*

J for Jade? Maybe it was a stretch, but it was certainly a possibility. She turned the page and read the entries more carefully. And then she saw it—*Cookout with J.* Under that was another list.

Hot dogs
Make buns
Baked beans
M – potato salad
C – beets & pickles
R – dessert

That was all the confirmation she needed. Francie, Caroline, Minnie, and Roxy had held a cookout with Jade. Not the whole scout troop. Was that the same day they'd taken the photograph? Or had it been a regular thing? Considering Francie's note about taking food to "J," it was likely they frequently met at the camp to have meals with Jade.

She kept going, then stopped at words she'd seen before. *Star Finder Badge* was written across the top. A horizontal line was drawn across the middle of the page. The top portion was labeled *42*, the bottom *RJCM*.

RJCM. Roxy, Jade, Caroline, Minnie.

Four things were listed on each half. In the top section:

- *Cincinnati Observatory (Birthplace of American Astronomy) – Edith will research and report*
- *Swasey Observatory, Granville – Shirley's family will visit. Report on 10/2*
- *Constellation maps*
- *Star watching until midnight at Dennison Park – Friday*

The second section sounded much more fun.

- *Overnight at Camp S*
- *Make papier-mâché solar system mobile*
- *Chart moon phases through July*
- *Act out Andromeda story—*
  Andromeda – J
  Cepheus – C
  Sea monster – M
  Perseus – R

Debbie had to laugh at the thought of Jade playing the beautiful princess who had to be chained to a rock to save her life and Minnie as the ferocious sea creature slithering around her.

Two lists. One for the official scout troop, the other for…a secret troop?

"Francie, you must have been an amazing woman. Wish I could have met you."

The doorbell rang. As she got up to answer it, she whispered to the empty room, "If you were still here, I think you'd be the kind of wild and crazy adventurer who'd put corn on pizza."

CHAPTER FOURTEEN

"This is actually delicious." Julian held up a piece of corn-topped pizza as if he were making a toast to Suki.

Suki, clearly much more relaxed in their company than she had been two nights earlier, laughed. "I believe the American response to that is 'I told you so.'"

The table erupted in laughter, and Julian held up his hand for a high five.

"You're going to fit in fine here," Debbie said.

The sweet smile faltered. "I hope you are right." Suki's voice was low and tight.

Debbie glanced at Jaxon and caught the grimace he quickly hid. "Did something happen last night at the meeting?" If so, she would be sure to let Ashling know.

"No, the meeting was lovely. It was this afternoon. I went to the pool with Mindy and some of her friends. I think Mrs. Porter made her invite me. I—" She blinked fast. "I do not think it was Mindy's idea to take in a foreign exchange student."

"Can you tell me what happened?"

Suki shrugged. "They acted like I wasn't even there. I got in the pool, but when I came out, they were all whispering. So I left. I tried walking back to the Porters', but I got lost, so I called Jaxon and..." A tear slid down her cheek. "I was so excited about school starting. I expected that it would be hard being the new girl, but never like this."

Debbie locked eyes with Greg. She had no words. Would Suki be made to feel that way for the rest of the school year?

"I'm sorry you had to deal with that, Suki," Jaxon said. "There are always mean kids, but I'll make sure you meet some of the good ones before school starts. We'll stick by you. I promise. Okay?"

Debbie watched as Greg's expression of helplessness transformed into unmistakable pride.

Suki straightened, and her smile returned. "Thank you. All of you. I have been thinking about the verse Jaxon asked me to translate, and it has brought me comfort. But for now, we cannot let the pizza get cold. And let's get on with the mystery. I have things to tell you."

As they ate, Suki repeated the things she had learned. "My grandfather's friend, Mr. Saito, located information about a Tanaka family from Los Angeles in the records he has compiled and also in files kept by the US War Relocation Authority. Tanaka is a common name, but this family was fined by the US government because their daughter, Jade Aimi Tanaka, was not with them when they were picked up for the trip to Gila River War Relocation Center. They claimed their daughter had run away."

Had Roxy Britton harbored a fugitive from the US government? Usually, Debbie couldn't condone such a thing, but in this case, she couldn't say that she wouldn't have done the exact same thing.

"He also found a sponsorship document signed by Luanne Britton, dated September of 1942. She was sponsoring Kenji and Miko Tanaka so that they could be released from the camp."

Debbie leaned back, feeling like she'd read the last page of a happily-ever-after book. "But where did they live? No one I've talked to remembers Jade living in Dennison." The question was rhetorical, answered only by pondering silence.

"Jaxon tells me you and your friend are amateur sleuths," Suki said. "I would love to hear about your cases."

Debbie resisted the urge to smile at Jaxon. She'd take it as a good sign that he'd talked about her in a way that seemed positive. "Dennison may appear to be a quiet little town, but we do have our share of mysteries and adventures. And you've already been a huge help with this one."

While they finished their pizza, they talked of lighter things, and Debbie promised to take Suki shopping for a sleeping bag and hiking boots the next day, since Mrs. Porter had an appointment and couldn't take her. She cleared plates and took them into the kitchen, then returned with the doughnuts she'd brought home from the café.

The kids' reaction to Janet's 1942 recipe for Salvation Army doughnuts did not disappoint. Suki ate two, and the boys each wolfed down three. When Debbie offered to bring out some more, Greg told her, "If they have any more sugar, I'm leaving them with you."

Debbie tapped her chin with her index finger. "I was thinking about cleaning out the garage since it's a little cooler today. I could use a few extra hands."

Julian laughed. "In that case, three's good."

When Debbie stood and picked up the empty tray, Suki stood too. "May I help you?"

There wasn't much cleanup to be done, so she was about to refuse, but a gut feeling told her the girl needed to talk to her about something.

So instead of sticking the dishes in the dishwasher, she filled the sink, handed Suki a dish towel, and began washing. "Do the Porters have any trips planned this year?" She hoped Suki's host family planned to show her more of the US—and that the question wouldn't cause more distress.

"Next week we are going to Chicago. I have been reading a travel book. Chicago sounds exciting." But her voice didn't reflect the excitement she spoke of.

"Do you get along okay with Mindy's little sister?"

Now the smile returned. "Jilly is so sweet. It is hard to understand how two sisters can be so different." She covered her lips with her fingertips. "I shouldn't say that."

Debbie rinsed a plate under hot water then shut off the tap and faced Suki. "It's all right to be honest about your feelings. One thing that helps me deal with difficult people is trying to understand why they are the way they are." She hesitated for a moment, then decided to take her own advice and be transparent. "The story we heard last night about Morgan and Macy's grandmother actually helped me a great deal."

Suki's forehead creased. "How?"

"Their grandmother is a food critic, someone whose job is to go into restaurants and tell people exactly what they think about the service and the food. She had some things to say about our café that were difficult to hear."

Understanding lit Suki's face. "I do not know anything about who or what might have hurt Mindy. But maybe I need to listen more. Between the lines, yes?"

Debbie smiled at her. "Yes, exactly. It's hard, when you feel you're being attacked, but I think God may have sent you to the Porters for such a time as this."

"Like Esther." Suki beamed. "Thank you. I think I can do this. And I think you can too."

"I'm going to try. But for now"—she winked as she used the exact words Suki had used earlier—"let's get on with the mystery."

When they returned to the table, the boys asked to see everything Debbie had found in the scout handbook again. While they arranged them on the table and kept up a comical running commentary on each item, Suki leafed through the book, occasionally stopping to ask for help with a word. "Did girls really learn all of this?"

"I doubt they all tried to earn all of the badges," Debbie said, "but yes, they had the opportunity to do so."

Suki turned a page then flipped back several pages. "What are all these letters circled?"

Her question stopped the boys' chatter. "Letters?" Jaxon scooted his chair closer. Julian picked up his chair and moved to Suki's left.

"Starting here"—she paged back—"there are letters and numbers circled in pencil on almost every page."

As if choreographed, Greg and Debbie stood at the same time and leaned in behind the kids.

"Whoa." Julian let out a low whistle as Suki turned pages and pointed to tiny, almost imperceptible circles.

"That has to be some sort of code, right?" Jaxon said.

"Ashling mentioned smudges on the pages about the Star Finder Badge. I didn't think anything about it," Debbie admitted. "I feel kind of silly that I haven't paid much attention to the book itself. I was focused on what was stuck inside."

Jaxon reached for Debbie's notebook and pen. "Read them out loud."

Suki went to the page where the circles began. "There's something written up in the corner."

Greg bent closer. "It's those numbers we've been seeing, 5:44."

"The Bible verse." Debbie leaned over Julian and pointed to the business card with Matthew 5:44 written on it in Japanese. "Maybe the letters spell out the verse."

Jaxon began writing the circled letters and numbers as Suki read them to him. She'd read at least a dozen when she stopped. "This is the first one capitalized. That might be important."

When they finished, Jaxon read the letters and numbers he'd written down out loud. "516no005mlehteeMecilopllaCniart225 potsgninnalPgnihctawneM."

A frustrated sigh came from Julian. "It's just a bunch of gibberish. It doesn't spell anything."

"Maybe we need a key to decipher it." Greg suggested.

Julian pulled the book toward him and found the page where the circles started. "5:44." Then he flipped to the page with the last circle and pointed at the page number.

The other four gasped in unison. The circles ended on page 544.

"So what if"—Jaxon put his fingertip on the line he'd written—"what if 544 is where the message *begins*."

"Like traditional Japanese," Suki added. "Read right to left."

Jaxon moved his finger slowly from the end of the line, murmuring the words as he did. "'Men watching Planning stop 522 train Call police Meet helm 500 on 615.'" He pumped his right fist in the air.

"Helm," Debbie echoed. "Jupiter's Helm is the name of a cave at Camp Saundustee."

"The 522 train is easy," Julian said. "That would be the train scheduled at the depot at 5:22, right?"

"Most likely," Greg answered. "So what is 615? Another time of day? Date?"

"It says 'on 615,'" Jaxon said. "Seems like it would be a date, probably June fifteenth."

Debbie tempered her smile as she relished the spark of adventure in Jaxon's voice. "So now we need to ask Kim to look at records from 1942 and find out who or what was on that train."

"And who were the men who planned to stop it," Jaxon added.

Julian gave a dramatically maniacal laugh that reverberated in the room. "And whether the Girl Scouts poisoned them before they could?"

Dennison, Ohio
June 3, 1942

Roxy sat cross-legged on the twin bed closest to the window in the room she shared with Caroline. Lightning forked across an inky-black sky that felt like the middle of the night instead of midafternoon. Her diary lay open in her lap. Since Sunday, she'd tried to record everything about Jade's arrival, but she had to do it in a way that the two younger girls giggling in the room across the hall couldn't decipher.

At ten, her little sister was beginning to be curious about everything the "big girls" did. Diana and her best friend, Gayle Zink, had started dressing like Roxy and Caroline, copying their slang and mannerisms and trying to eavesdrop on every conversation. When she was younger, Roxy had often heard her mother use the phrase "Little pitchers have big ears." It made no sense to her at the time, even when her mother pointed out the ear-shaped handle on the cream pitcher.

Now she understood.

She wrote the date across the top of the page then began to write.

Planning a cookout tomorrow night. Minnie's granddad made hot dogs for us. Hope to get there early enough to walk around the perimeter of the camp again, checking for prints or other signs that would explain some of the sounds we've heard during the day. Thankfully, whatever is prowling out there is not nocturnal.

What would she remember if she read over this entry years in the future? Would she remember sitting in this very room, writing words that two little girls couldn't understand even if they used a paper clip to unlock her diary? Would she remember the chill of fear she and Jade had felt several times now when the sound of an ax or hammer echoed through the trees? Would she recall Jade's pale face when she'd said she was sure she'd heard men yelling not far from her cabin?

Lord, if I've put Jade in danger, please, please show us what to do. Please protect her. *It was a prayer she'd uttered over and over in the past two days. Especially today, when rain pelted the windows and she was forced to stay home. She felt helpless. She couldn't check on Jade, so she had no idea how she was doing alone in a storm. Jade was the most resourceful girl she knew, but everyone had limits, especially with legitimate reasons to be afraid.*

She set aside her diary and picked up the letter she'd written that morning. She couldn't put it in the mailbox, not even next door at her house. Couldn't take a chance on anyone seeing the envelope addressed to Rev. and Mrs. Kenji Tanaka in care of the Gila River War Relocation Center in Arizona. She couldn't even trust their mailman. Even though Mr. Hill was one of the nicest men she knew, he was friends with Mr. Davis. How easy it would be for him to ask an innocent question that could put Jade in danger.

She reread the letter and prayed it wouldn't be intercepted at Gila River and that Jade's parents would understand it.

Dear Uncle Ken and Aunt Miko,

Just wanted you to know we received the gift you sent Mom. It arrived in perfect condition. We set it in a place of honor, and it appears to be working fine.

My last day as a sophomore was last week. I am so excited to have a whole summer stretched out ahead to spend with my oldest friend. Her mother is a bit of a worrier, so we can't do anything too wild and crazy, but I do hope to have some adventures to tell when I go back to school.

My latest letter from Dad came two weeks ago. He couldn't tell me where he was, but he sounded well. So very much to pray about.

I hope you are well. I was sad to learn you had to move. I pray every night that this war ends soon. My Girl Scout troop is doing what we can to help. We have planted a large Victory Garden outside of town. I loved the planting part, but I'm sure the weeding will not be quite so fun. We are also helping at the train depot where soldiers arrive at all times of the day and night. We hand out sandwiches and drinks and doughnuts. Some of the men are only two years older than I am. I want to cry when I think of what this horrible war is doing to families. My heart aches for all the mothers who are separated from their children.

I don't know if it is possible for you to write back, but please know that I will write to you every week.

All my love,

Roxy

This was her second draft. In the first, she'd written that her mother was working at Walter Reed and would be home at the end of the month. She'd said she and Diana were staying with the Davises and that "the gift" was safe.

Then she'd had second thoughts. She didn't like the idea of letting Jade's parents think their daughter was staying at the Davises when she wasn't. Would Aunt Miko worry that they were imposing on the neighbor? Or worse, had Mom ever told her about Mr. Davis and the way he belittled his wife and daughter? In all possibility, she may have mentioned living next to an angry bigoted man. So she'd ripped up the first try and rewritten it. All Jade's parents needed to know was that their daughter was safe. Roxy prayed that was the truth.

She wouldn't put a return address on the envelope. Tomorrow she'd walk to the post office and wait until the lobby was full of people opening their mailboxes and waiting in line. Then she'd duck inside and slide the envelope in the slot. No one would know. She folded the page and tucked it into an envelope. As she was licking the flap, giggles reached her ears.

"Writing to a boy, Roxy?" Diana's singsong came from the hallway.

"Are you in loooove, Roxy?" Gayle chanted, in the same grating voice. "We can steam it open, you know."

The two girls giggled.

She smiled at them, knowing that if she expressed any frustration, it would merely make them more curious. "Not today, Nancy Drews."

Tonight she'd sleep with her diary and the envelope under her pillow.

CHAPTER FIFTEEN

Debbie woke an hour before her alarm was set to go off on Friday morning. After a leisurely time of prayer and Bible reading, she got ready for work then sat back at the kitchen table with the Girl Scout box.

"Tell me more, Francie." She opened the notebook and found where she'd left off. The page had *JCMR Overnight* written at the top. Under it was a to-do list with things like *Find jacket for J* and *Bake blueberry muffins*. The "Bring" list was much longer, consisting mostly of ingredients for beef stew. *Soup pot, stew meat, potatoes, carrots, onion, flour, cutting board, knife, spoons, bowls.*

"I'm impressed, Francie. Making stew from scratch over an open fire." She read the rest of the list. *Eggs, lemonade, picnic bucket cooler.* That last item resurrected a long-forgotten memory. She was a little girl, maybe no more than five, when her grandparents had taken her to an outdoor movie. Grandma had filled her vintage, red plaid metal cooler with ice and glass bottles of soda "the way we did it in the old days." She'd sat in the front seat between her grandparents, eating popcorn and sipping soda from a glass bottle while they watched…actually, she wasn't sure which movie they'd watched. What she remembered was the company, and she was glad.

The memory, along with the book in front of her, sent her down a rabbit hole of nostalgia.

So much had changed in the past eighty-plus years. Life had been harder in the forties for everyone, but in so many ways it had also been simpler. Francie didn't have the convenience of fast food, but she lived in an era when families sitting down together for meals was the norm. She wouldn't have been able to email or text the girls in her troop with reminders, but when she spoke to them, she'd have their full attention. "I kind of envy you," Debbie murmured.

She turned another page. This one was headed, *Help with Fly-Up Ceremony*. Below it was a list of Junior Scouts who would be moving up to become Cadettes. Two names grabbed her attention—Diana Britton and Gayle Zink.

Was Gayle still in town? Maybe she could drop by after work. But she had promised to take Suki shopping for camping supplies. She'd have to come up with something else.

As an idea took shape, she glanced at the clock. Her dad would have been up and moving for an hour by now, either out for a walk with one of his neighbors or getting ready for a round of golf. He'd mentioned a few days ago that he wanted to treat a couple of his favorite Good Shepherd residents to lunch sometime soon. She called him, smiling when she heard his voice.

"What are you doing for lunch today, Dad?"

"I know that tone." He gave a long sigh, loaded with fake exasperation. "I suppose I'm doing whatever my daughter wants me to do."

"You mentioned wanting to take Ray and Eileen out for lunch one of these days."

"I did. And I take it you've decided that today would be a good day, but I have to wonder why."

"Because they love getting out," she said, trying to sound as innocent as possible.

"Debbie, I raised you," he reminded her.

She gave it up. "And I want to pick their brains about the things I found in the old Girl Scout book. The two of them together might remember more than if I talked to each one separately. Though they really do love to get out. Did Mom tell you about the book?" She'd had a brief conversation about it with her mother but hadn't mentioned it to her dad yet.

"A little. Something about a poisonous flower and a movie ticket."

"You're intrigued, aren't you? And you want to know more, right?"

"Right." He chuckled. "I'll call them. Anything else I can do for you?"

"Well, since you asked, how'd you like to pick up Ray's sister, Gayle, from her cousin's house?"

Another laugh. "Your mother has this crazy belief that I can't say no to you. No idea where she gets that."

"Me neither. That's ridiculous. See you for lunch," Debbie said brightly.

The rain was a nice reprieve from the heat, but after several hours of customers dashing into the café with damp shirts and hair, it was beginning to feel like a sauna. After clearing the last table, Debbie leaned against the counter and stared out at the gray sky. Her weather app promised that the clouds would dissipate by nightfall, and tomorrow would be a gorgeous blue-sky day with temperatures in the midseventies, lowering to the sixties after the sun went down. A perfect combination for stargazing.

When the late-morning lull hit, Debbie walked over to the museum with a doughnut and coffee for Kim, which the curator received with enthusiasm. Then she showed Kim the code they'd found in the handbook.

"Intriguing." Kim's eyes sparkled with the same excitement Debbie had felt yesterday as they'd deciphered the message. She took a slip of paper and wrote *5:22 train. June 15, 1942.* "We have schedules and records going back a lot further than that. I don't know how soon I can get to it, but I hope I can find something that helps. Any theories?"

"Nothing promising. If we're interpreting it right, how did a teenage girl find out someone was trying to stop a train?"

"Good question," Kim mused. "Girl Scouts volunteered here during the war. I wonder if the men they overheard talking about holding up a train could have been working here."

"That's possible."

Kim thanked her again for the goodies and promised to let Debbie know if she found anything.

As Debbie returned to the café, she saw her father's car pull into the parking lot. She held the front door of the depot open, and Gayle and Eileen walked in together, followed by her dad pushing Ray in his wheelchair. Debbie gave her father a hug.

"Hey, what does a guy have to do to get one of those?" asked the ninety-nine-year-old man in the wheelchair. His sister smacked his arm, giving Debbie a glimpse of the playfulness that may have characterized their relationship as children.

"He just has to be patient." Debbie leaned down and put her arms around Ray.

"For once, I didn't have to bribe this guy with lunch so he would spring me." Ray's eyes twinkled.

Debbie laughed. Her father had been the director of Good Shepherd Retirement Center for decades. Unlike people who never wanted to set foot in their former workplace after retirement, her father loved spending time with the residents at his. "You have me to thank for this one." She walked ahead of them to one of the tables best suited for a wheelchair and removed a chair to make room.

When Ray was in place, she bent down and said, in a conspiratorial whisper loud enough to be sure he heard her, "I have an in with the owners, so if said guy is really nice, they might give him a discount."

"That's why you have loyal customers, my dear. In spite of what some angry, unreasonable critics might be saying."

"You read food blogs?"

"I do now." His scowl broadcast exactly what he thought of the blog.

"That Gastro Gnome person has been the main topic of conversation at Good Shepherd," Eileen said. "Who in the world does she think she is?"

"Well, everyone is entitled to their own opinion, right?" Debbie rested a hand on Ray's shoulder. "One of the things our armed forces have fought for is our First Amendment rights."

"True," Ray agreed. "But I wish those rights weren't hurting you and Janet."

"Ray showed me those awful reviews, and I admire your attitude," Gayle said. "Our mother was fond of quoting Proverbs 19:11. 'The discretion of a man deferreth his anger; and it is his glory to pass over a transgression.'"

Debbie had learned that one too but in a more modern version. *A person's wisdom yields patience; it is to one's glory to overlook an offense.* "Actually, we're grateful for Gastro Gnome's opinions because our regulars, and even some people who've only been here when they were passing through, have written some glowing comments in response. We've been busier than ever this week."

"Good to hear."

Her father pulled out chairs for Gayle and Eileen. Debbie brought them water and menus then took their orders. When their food was ready, things were still slow enough that she could take some time to chat.

She took the Girl Scout book out of her purse and tucked it under her arm before picking up their plates. After making sure they had everything they needed, she sat next to her dad and closed her eyes while he offered a blessing.

Then she dove in right away. "I found something I want to ask you all about, but I guess I need to start at the beginning." She set the handbook on the table and told them about finding it in the storeroom. As soon as she mentioned Roxy's name, Gayle's eyes lit. "Did you have something to say about Roxy, Gayle?" she asked.

"I suppose you already know Roxy became a famous children's author. I heard she had cancer. So sad."

"I hadn't heard that," Eileen said. "But she's leaving a beautiful written legacy behind." So like Eileen to focus on the good.

Gayle gazed off in the distance for a moment, her expression muted, but the smile returned quickly. "Yes, she is. Roxy's sister, Diana, was my best friend in grade school. We drove Roxy and her friend Caroline crazy, always following them around and trying to listen in on their conversations."

Anticipation surged through Debbie's veins. "Did you ever meet Jade Tanaka?"

"No. But I heard about her visit. I was away at college when Roxy and Jade came to Dennison. I wish I could have seen Roxy again and met Jade. Diana talked a lot about her family friends, the Tanakas, when we were little."

"But you never heard anything about Jade being in Dennison during the war?"

"Well, yes, now that I think about it. I suppose that was during the Korean War."

"Sorry. I didn't make that clear. Did you ever hear anything about Jade being here in 1942?"

Gayle's eyes widened with an expression that said that was a ridiculous question. "Jade's family was in a detention camp during the war. I remember Diana talking about how sad it was. She said the camps were uninsulated, lacked running water, were ringed with barbed wire, and patrolled by armed guards. I think her mother was writing letters to try to get them out."

Debbie opened the book and pulled out a piece of paper. She slid the photocopied picture in front of Gayle. "A note on the back of the original said it was taken on June 28, 1942, at Camp Saundustee."

Squinting, Gayle picked it up in a gnarled hand that trembled slightly. "That's impossible. But that's Francie Reese, the Girl Scout leader, and Roxy. And Caroline and Minnie. How on earth?" The confusion on Gayle's face made Debbie fear she'd made the woman question if her memory was failing.

Eileen patted Gayle's hand. "I'm sure there's some mistake. The camp didn't open until after the war. I do remember meeting Jade in the fifties. She talked about living in Chicago. Her father worked for a publishing house, and she went to college there." She tapped the photo. "See the date on the edge of the photograph? This was developed in 1948."

"The note on the back said it was taken in 1942," Debbie said. "We thought they might have waited to develop the film."

"I can easily understand how the date could be incorrect," Ray said. "I've gone through old photos and tried to figure out when they were taken by studying things in the background. It's easy to be off by several years. I remember meeting Jade too. In a strange place on June 22, 1956." He tapped his temple. "How's that for a sharp memory?"

Eileen laughed, and Gayle gave a sound something like a snort. "It was your birthday," the two said in unison.

"Yup. A buddy and his wife had invited me for supper to celebrate. I'd just gotten out of my car out on Saundustee Road, when here come four grown women on bicycles." He laid a gnarled finger on the photocopied picture and turned it toward him. "Minnie, Caroline, Roxy, and a woman with jet-black hair I would definitely have remembered meeting before."

"They were riding on Saundustee Road?" Debbie asked.

Ray gave a slow nod. "About a mile from the camp."

"We think those girls and Francie hid Jade at Saundustee in 1942."

"*Hid*?" Three voices chorused together.

"We don't know how she got here or if she ran away from the detention camp or was sent here by her parents."

Gayle tapped her fingers on the table and gazed past Debbie as if trying to remember those days. "I haven't thought of this in eighty years, but there was a time when the big girls were going to ride their bikes out to Camp Saundustee for a picnic. Diana and I begged to go along, but Mrs. Davis said we were too young to ride that far. Finally, she gave in and said she would drive us, but Roxy and Caroline had a fit, saying we couldn't be trusted not to fall off a cliff or get lost in the cave or bitten by rattlesnakes." She smiled. "Their arguments were so far-fetched that we all ended up laughing hysterically. I think Mrs. Davis ended up taking us to Tappan Lake that day instead."

"That could support my theory," Debbie said.

Gayle rested against the back of the chair. "They were always acting secretive, and we knew they were up to something, but I can't believe they were hiding Jade and we never knew it."

"Sounds like Caroline's parents didn't know either," Ray said. "Things were different then. In summer, so many kids left the house after breakfast and only came home for meals until bedtime."

"Do you remember overhearing the girls talk about what some bad men were doing, maybe having something to do with trying to hold up a train?" Debbie asked Gayle.

The woman's face pinched. "I don't remember any talk about bad men, but they were definitely keeping something from us. Roxy had a diary. It had a lock, but it was easy to pick. She hid it in a different place every night, but that didn't stop us. At first it was silly stuff about boys and movie stars and how much she missed her parents, but then it was like she started writing in code or something. Not an actual code, but things that didn't make any sense."

"Like what?" Debbie asked eagerly.

"The one specific thing I remember overhearing was one time when Diana and Madeline and I followed the big girls into town. We were pretending to be spies, so we took the alleys and kept watching for them between houses. They went to the drugstore, but instead of sitting at the counter like they usually did, they went to the pay phone in the back. We hid behind a shelf while Roxy made a call. We made out something about stealing sugar but not much else. I thought Roxy was tattling on Diana to their mother, but Diana said she hadn't taken any sugar. Then Minnie joined them outside and asked if they'd called the police, and they said yes."

Debbie gave a slow nod. "That fills in a few blanks."

Gayle's thin lips pressed together. "Do you think calling the police had something to do with Jade?"

"I think it had something to do with a train robbery. There was a newspaper clipping in the guidebook about four tons of sugar being stolen from a train car at the depot."

"Goodness. So Roxy and Caroline were reporting it?"

Debbie opened the book and pointed out the circled letters and numbers, then unzipped the bag of clues and showed them the newspaper article and the paper with the deciphered message.

"They knew about it before it happened." Ray let out a low whistle. "How?"

"I don't know."

Gayle tapped a fingertip on the article. "But they were too late, weren't they? They didn't stop the robbery."

"For some reason, calling the police didn't work," Debbie said. "But why?"

CHAPTER SIXTEEN

"'ll pick you up in fifteen." Debbie untied her apron and tossed it into the laundry as she darted toward the door on Saturday afternoon. "Is Tiffany going with us?"

Janet tugged off her own apron. "She went ahead with Ashling, and Ian will join us after work. All I have to do is change clothes and grab the muffins."

They parted ways, Janet driving off and Debbie sprinting home. She was out of breath when she unlocked her front door. Upstairs, she changed into shorts and a T-shirt. She'd have to put on long pants before nightfall, but it was too hot to think about that now. After double-checking her pack, she carried it down to the kitchen then ran through her lists. Like Francie, she had a "To Do" list and a "To Bring" list. Unlike Francie, the hot dog buns she'd offered to bring had come from the store, not her oven.

In ten minutes she'd loaded the car with her backpack, camp chair, hiking boots, sleeping bag, pillow, and food, and was on her way to Janet's. As she pulled up in front of the Shaw house, her phone rang. Madeline O'Sullivan's name flashed on the screen. Debbie closed her eyes as she answered, shielding herself against bad news. "Hello?"

"Debbie, I just got a call from Diana. Roxy's pastor came to see her, so they lowered her morphine enough for them to have a final conversation. She's awake and pretty clearheaded. Diana told her how you found her Girl Scout book and have some questions about it, and she wants to talk to you."

"That's incredible. Is she with Roxy now?"

"Yes. She told me to give you her phone number. It sounds like right now is a good time if you're free."

Debbie dug through her purse for a pen and a scrap of paper and wrote down the number. After saying goodbye, she texted Janet. ON THE PHONE WITH ROXY.

As she tapped in the number, it occurred to her that all the questions she'd had for the past week could be answered with this one call. Instead of searching for clues at the Star Party, she could be recounting Jade's story around the campfire.

"Hello. This is Diana." The voice, though slightly shaky, sounded warm and friendly.

"Hi, this is Debbie Albright. I found your sister's Girl Scout handbook," Debbie said.

"How lovely to hear from you. I was hoping you'd be able to call. I'm sitting here with my sister, and she is very intrigued about what you've discovered. I'll put you on speakerphone. Okay, go ahead."

"Thank you. Hi Roxy. I co-own the Whistle Stop Café located in the old train depot in Dennison, Ohio. A young friend of ours just became a Girl Scout leader, and I remembered seeing an old handbook in a display in our museum. We found it, and it had your name in it. There are all sorts of intriguing things stuck between the pages."

"The flower?" The weak, trembly voice had to be Roxy's.

"Yes. I've been very careful with it. We didn't touch it."

"Good. What else?" Roxy asked in a husky whisper.

"There was a newspaper clipping about a shipment of sugar being stolen, what appeared to be a constellation map, and a Bible verse written in Japanese. Oh, and a movie ticket. It said something on the back about disguising 'J' and sneaking her in."

Was that a laugh?

"I don't think I heard about that one," Diana said. "No one can keep secrets like my sister."

Janet came out of the house, and Debbie popped the trunk open. She started to ask another question when she heard something too quiet for her make out the words. "I'm sorry, I didn't quite catch that."

"She wants to know what you've figured out," Diana said.

"Well, after talking to Madeline and Gayle, then finding a notebook that belonged to Francie Reese—" She stopped at the sound of a gasp. "Goodness. Is everything all right?"

"All those names are making Roxy a bit emotional." The quaver in Diana's voice said her sister wasn't alone in that. "Go ahead, dear."

"We think Jade Tanaka somehow got to Dennison in 1942, where Roxy, Caroline Davis, and Minnie Franklin hid her out at Camp Saundustee with Francie's help. We also think they found out about the plans to steal the sugar from the boxcar at the depot, but either they were too late, or the authorities didn't act quickly enough to stop it."

"She's smiling and shaking her head," Diana reported. "Roxy, can you set them straight?"

"Soon." Roxy sounded weaker than she had been moments before. "It will all be clear soon."

"I'm sorry. She seems to be done talking for right now." Diana's voice was louder. She'd shut off speakerphone. "I wish I could fill in the details for you, but I've never heard about the boxcar. You're right about them hiding Jade, though. I didn't find that out until the two of them were together some years ago. You can imagine what a shock that was. Gayle and I knew the big girls were hiding something. I never would have guessed it was a some*one*."

Janet opened the passenger door and slid into the seat, pulling the door closed as quietly as she could.

Debbie put her phone on speaker. "Is Jade still alive, by any chance?"

Diana gave the answer Debbie had expected. "Sadly, no. She passed away a year ago in Nagoya, Japan, where she and her husband were missionaries for more than forty years. She had an amazing life and left a beautiful legacy of faith for generations to come."

"That's what we all wish for, isn't it?"

"It is. Now, I'll try to answer any questions you have, but I'm afraid I've been kept in the dark about much of this story."

"Do you know how long Jade stayed out at Camp Saundustee?"

"I don't. Our mother was working at Walter Reed Hospital at the time. Oh, how I wish I'd asked more questions. I don't know how long we stayed with the Davises. We were there when school got out and for part of the summer. I do remember that when Mom came home, I barely had time to hug her before Roxy pulled her into my dad's office. They whispered in there for a long time, and then Mom sent me back to the Davises' while she and Roxy went somewhere. I was crushed, but now I know they went out to see Jade."

"Did they bring her to your house?"

"No. I never saw her. I assume a ten-year-old couldn't be trusted to keep a secret. Like I said, I didn't know anything about her being in Dennison until a few years ago. Not a word was said in my presence. I wish I'd known about this when my mother was still living. She might have been more forthcoming than my sister. I do know she arranged something for Jade and her family, but I don't have details of that."

"I can fill in a couple of blanks. A friend of a friend who has done research on families who were confined found sponsorship papers with Jade's parents' names on them. They were signed by your mother. And one of our older residents, Eileen Palmer, said she met Jade in the fifties. Jade told her she'd gone to college in Chicago."

"I suppose Chicago would have been a more accepting place. Mother had a friend there who was married to a pastor. I suppose she could have arranged something with them."

"Maybe this is too nosy, but why do you think Roxy hasn't told you about the men who stole the sugar? I can't help but wonder if there was more to that story."

"I have no idea. After all this time, I can't imagine any reason for secrecy. I will say that the last time I was with Jade and my sister, I felt like a ten-year-old again, sneaking around and trying to figure out what they were talking about. The two of them had this ability to know what the other was saying when it didn't make sense to anyone else in the room."

"Gayle mentioned that Roxy had a diary during that time. Do you know if she kept it?"

"Oh yes. She has an entire safe full of diaries. I don't know if anyone has the combination, though. I'm hoping she's given it to her attorney or her agent so someone can read them someday." Diana chuckled. "Gayle and I tried at the time, but we couldn't make heads or tails of any of it."

"That's what she said as well. I won't keep you. Thank you for your time. I know it's particularly precious right now. I'll be praying for Roxy. And you."

"Thank you, dear. If I can get Roxy to divulge anything else and give me permission to share it with you, I will. And if you learn anything new, please let me know."

"I will."

Debbie ended the call, feeling discouraged. "I'm afraid the truth may pass away with Roxy."

As they stood in the middle of the circle of cabins at Camp Saundustee, Debbie handed out copies of the constellation map from Roxy's handbook—one to Janet and Ian, another to Suki, Macy, and Morgan. She kept the third for herself and Greg. "You're sure your grandma doesn't want to join us?" she asked the twins.

"Walking in the woods is, uh, not really her thing." Morgan pointed to her feet and then Macy's. They both wore long pants, too warm for the weather, tucked into heavy socks. "Ticks. Among other creepy-crawly things."

"She's happy to wait in the air-conditioned building until everyone else gets here." Macy added.

Janet took Ian's hand. "Team Shaw for the win!"

"No way." Morgan waved their map in the air. "Girls rule! We're definitely going to figure this out first."

"Okay." Debbie laughed. "Team Shaw, you stay here in Maple Ridge. Team Girls Rule, you've got Cloud Crest, and Team—"

"AC," Greg suggested. "A for Albright, C for Connor."

"I like it. It also makes me think about air-conditioning."

"Because we're so cool?" Greg asked with a grin.

She groaned. "We'll take Hickory Haven. We have no idea what we're looking for, so do a thorough search of the tent or cabin marked by a star on your map. Take pictures if you find anything that might be of interest. Let's try to be back here in time to help with supper."

The girls took off at a run, and Janet and Ian headed toward the designated cabin.

Greg held out his hand, and she took it. "All jokes aside, I like us being on the same team."

"So do I."

They walked along the grassy path in comfortable silence. Debbie felt laughter rising in her throat when a memory took her by surprise. She and Janet had taken this exact route three times a day, to the dining hall and back, when they were at camp. On many of those walks they'd chatted about boys. Sometimes it would be about a particular boy, but more often it centered around the qualities they would look for in a boy when they were old enough to "go out." One year, they'd made lists and read them to each other on the way to breakfast. She remembered a few of the things on her list: *Must love Jesus, animals, nature, children, and his mom. And must make me laugh.*

Somehow, she'd found a man who checked all of those boxes.

As they walked into the Hickory Haven unit between two platform tents, Debbie again felt as if she'd stepped back in time. Nothing had changed. The circle of tents, the rocks around the firepit. No electricity. They could have been back in her scouting days—or even the end of Roxy's.

Greg unfolded the map he'd stuck in his pocket. His arm pressed lightly against hers as he held it in front of her. "Northwest corner." He pointed at the star on the map then at one of the tents. "I think it's that one."

"The popular girls stayed there." Debbie wasn't sure she wanted to share the details of her foray into the world of mean girls. The summer she played a part in crushing Sara Loring's spirit. What if it changed how Greg saw her?

She untied the tent flaps and stepped inside. The smell hadn't changed in thirty years. Canvas heating in the sun. A hint of mildew. Old wood. The bunks were bare. Days ago, the floor was likely littered with backpacks and shoes. Wet swimsuits would have hung from nails pounded into bunk frames. She hoped that true friendships had been forged in this space, and respect and kindness had reigned, as had happened in her day.

Shining her light along the floor and the four-by-four boards that held the canvas, she read names and dates. She tapped her foot on the wood beneath her. "If I remember right, the wood was fairly new when Janet and I were here, not like it had been here for forty-some years. I'm guessing it's all been replaced since the forties, so if whatever they were marking was a clue in the wood, it's probably long gone."

"Probably. Pressure-treating wood with chromated arsenicals started in the forties, but it's likely these were originally built with untreated wood that wouldn't have lasted. I doubt any of the wood is original. So whatever we're searching for is probably gone. The frustrating thing is that we don't actually know what we're searching for, so it's not safe to say either way."

"I know, but I'm not ready to give up yet." Debbie walked out ahead of him. While he retied the tent flaps, she stepped around the corner, to the side of the tent mostly hidden by sumac and tall grass. Pushing the brush aside, she found what she hadn't dared search for when she'd been here with Ashling, Tiffany, and Janet.

D.A.

The last in a line of initials. A line that started with *2P '93*. She could still clearly remember the sense of awe when she'd finished etching her name into the wood and the other girls clapped. She'd made it. She was an official member of "Perfect and Pretty." That euphoric feeling hadn't lasted a full day.

The memory almost made her queasy. Did any of Mindy Porter's friends feel the way she had, as if they were standing on the outside watching someone else's life? Laughing when they laughed, standing with one hand on their hip the way the others did. Even though her time near the top of the pecking order hadn't lasted long, every minute of it had felt stressful. Did she look right? Talk right? Walk right? Were any of the girls who'd picked on Suki feeling that same sick twist in their stomachs? Hating who they were but afraid of who they'd be without the approval of the girls they called friends—the same girls who would likely turn on them if they failed to meet their standards.

Maybe her memories would come in handy. If the Lord ever gave her an opportunity to talk to any of them, she needed to remember that they might not be as confident as they seemed, nor as mean as they tried to come across.

She stood and brushed off her knees. Why was this spot starred on the map? Was what they were searching for part of the original tent frame or something else? She walked around to the back of the tent and stared down into the valley. She couldn't see the waterfall from here, but sunlight glinted on the stream it fed. One of the counselors had explained that Saundustee meant "water," named by a tribe of Wyandotte American Indians who had once called this area home. On a clear night, like tonight would be, the sunset could be seen from every one of the units along the ridge surrounding the valley.

Greg came up behind her and rested his hands on her shoulders. "Gorgeous view."

"It sure is."

She stepped away from him with a bit of reluctance that was overshadowed by her excitement as she realized something. Clinging to a branch for support, she walked as close to the edge as she dared. The ground sloped away at about forty-five degrees. Walkable, but one misstep could result in a long tumble. "Down there, right in the middle of the valley. There used to be an old barn. It's gone, but—"

"The foundation is still standing," Greg finished for her.

"Now look around the ridge. What do you see?" She pointed at a spot of red next to a tent.

"Suki was wearing a red shirt, right?" The same excitement she felt was clear his voice.

"Yes. And there." She indicated a cabin along the top of the cliff.

"Is that the cabin Janet and Ian are checking out?"

"I think so." Seconds later, Janet's blond hair and bright-yellow shirt were visible as she rounded the corner.

"So the barn would have been visible from all three spots."

"Yep." She grinned up at him. "Hope you packed your hiking boots."

Dennison, Ohio
June 6, 1942

"Please, Daddy?" Caroline's most persuasive voice drifted up from downstairs. "It's a perfect night for stargazing. We're going to draw constellation maps and count how many shooting stars we see for our Star Finder badges."

Roxy lay on the floor in Caroline's bedroom with her ear pressed to the metal grate. Caroline was in her father's study directly below, arguing her case for another campout on the Camp Saundustee grounds. Sometimes she was sure Mr. Davis said no for no reason at all.

"You're gone too much. When I was your age, we didn't have summer vacation. We had summers off to work in the fields."

Roxy closed her eyes, hoping Caroline wouldn't remind him that they didn't own any fields.

"I know, Daddy," her friend said carefully. "We're very fortunate to have time for fun. All because you work so hard."

Hand over her mouth, Roxy held in the laugh that threatened to spill out.

"I just hope you're being smart," Mr. Davis grumbled. "Could be bums camping out in those woods."

"As often as we've been out there, I've never seen another human being."

Roxy grimaced. Caroline was telling the truth. They'd never seen another person. But someone was out there.

She hadn't told Caroline or Minnie about the sounds she and Jade heard. Or the footprints they'd found yesterday after a day of rain. Fresh prints near the old barn that had probably been built around the time of the Civil War. They hadn't been brave enough to peek between the weathered boards. It was likely being used as storage by the farmer who owned the corn field they could see through the trees, but they needed to check it out after dark when no one was around.

Mr. Davis harrumphed.

"The raspberries were almost ripe last week. I bet they're perfect now. I'll pick some and make raspberry icebox cake." Her tone was syrupy sweet. "Just like Grandma used to make."

Silence met Caroline's offer. Roxy watched the second hand on her watch make one complete revolution before Mr. Davis cleared his throat. "What did your mother say?"

"She said she was fine with us going if you were."

Roxy smiled. It wasn't a complete untruth. Mrs. Davis had said, "Talk to your father."

"If I let you do this, you and Roxanne are staying home all next week to help your mother paint the kitchen and dining room."

"Of course."

Roxy barely swallowed a groan, wishing Caroline had used her skills to bargain her way out of that. They couldn't leave Jade alone that long. Of course, Francie had offered to go out whenever Roxy couldn't, but it wasn't the same as seeing that her friend was all right with her own eyes.

"Well, then, you be home by ten for church. And take the big flashlights. I trust you, but I don't trust Roxanne not to do something foolish. You be the smart one, you hear?"

"Yes, Daddy," Caroline said. Did he not realize she only called him that when she wanted something? The kiss she likely planted on his scowling cheek resounded through the grate.

Ignoring the insult to her trustworthiness, Roxy jumped up and hung her green scarf in the window. A signal to Minnie, who was probably packed and waiting at the corner with her bike. By the time Caroline dashed up the stairs and into the room, Roxy had finished packing her rucksack.

Ten minutes later, they were on their way, pedaling as fast as they could on the gravel road. Usually, once they were on Saundustee Road, they never saw another vehicle. So when a gray flatbed pickup rumbled past them, Roxy shared the concern on Caroline's face. Three miles later, her heart skipped a beat.

Tire ruts in the still-muddy drive leading into the camp left no question. They were not alone.

CHAPTER SEVENTEEN

Debbie leaned back in her camp chair and folded her arms across her middle. The sky was a deep navy. More stars were becoming visible with each passing minute. The night was calm, and cool enough for her to welcome the warmth of a flannel shirt. She stared across the firepit at the man who stirred sparks from coals, as he also stirred sparks in her heart.

"People have been studying, writing stories and poems, and singing songs about the stars since history began." Greg glanced at his tablet as he addressed the group surrounding the campfire. "In the book of Amos in the Bible, we read, 'He who made the Pleiades and Orion, who turns midnight into dawn and darkens day into night, who calls for the waters of the sea and pours them out over the face of the land—the Lord is his name.' These words were written around 750 BC."

"And still as true now as they were then," Janet murmured.

"William Shakespeare called the stars 'blessed candles of the night,'" Greg went on. "And here's one of my favorites, from the twentieth century. Author Frances Clark said, 'There wouldn't be a sky full of stars if we were all meant to wish on the same one.'" His gaze swept the circle, landing for a fraction of a second on Suki with a hint of a smile in his eyes.

The girl beamed.

"We'll take a better look through the telescopes in a bit," Greg said. "But first, does anyone know what stars are made of?"

Two hands waved in the air, and he called on a girl with red curls. "Stars are made when dust clouds in a galaxy form tight knots that collapse under their own gravity. The collapse causes the middle of the cloud to get hot and start glowing. That's a baby star, or protostar."

Greg complimented the girl, added a bit to her description, and then began talking about constellations.

"More than a hundred years ago, in 1922, the International Astronomical Union created a list of eighty-eight officially recognized constellations. More than half of them were based on star drawings recorded by Ptolemy, a Greek astronomer in the second century. The constellations were named for legendary mythological characters like Perseus and his bride Andromeda. As the story goes, the beautiful princess Andromeda…"

The nostalgic feeling returned. Debbie had told Greg about finding Francie's notebook, but she hadn't shared details. He had no way of knowing that Roxy, Jade, Minnie, and Caroline had put on a play about the story he was telling right now. They could have performed it right here, in the middle of the circle of cabins.

She peered through the space beside the cabin marked with a star on Roxy's map. The waning light brushed the tips of trees on the other side of the valley. She couldn't see the barn's old stone foundation from here. Was the barn the reason for the map, as she suspected? And if so, why? Was it simply a game? Or somehow linked to the article about the stolen sugar or even the poisonous flower?

All questions had to wait until tomorrow morning. Janet had texted Sara and asked if several adults could explore the site of the old barn. She'd received an enthusiastic answer along with a warning. ABSOLUTELY! JUST WATCH OUT FOR RUSTY NAILS AND BROKEN GLASS.

Debbie brought her thoughts back to Greg.

"…but when Cassiopeia starts bragging that her daughter, Andromeda, is more beautiful than the sea nymphs, she enrages Poseidon. So Poseidon decides to get even by sending a sea monster to attack the king's country. When Cassiopeia and King Cepheus find out that the only way to save their land is to sacrifice their daughter to the sea creature, they chain Andromeda to a rock by the sea. But then the hero arrives to save the day! Perseus, son of Zeus, sees Andromeda while flying over the land with his winged sandals and falls in love with her. He asks her parents for permission to marry her if he's able to save her, and they agree. Then he kills the sea monster and rescues Andromeda, and they live happily ever after."

"Wow." The whisper came from right behind her, accompanied by a soft rustle, the sound of a camp chair opening. "He sure knows how to captivate an audience."

Not recognizing the female voice, Debbie swiveled and smiled at a blond-haired woman she didn't know, then faced forward again. "He sure does."

"Heard you two are dating," the woman said. The statement was followed by a congratulatory pat on her elbow.

Who was this person? If she tried to get a better view, she'd create a distraction. As it was, Janet was watching them. And smiling like she didn't think there was anything weird about a stranger showing up hours after the party had started and clapping a hand on Debbie's arm.

"So good to see you, Debbie," the woman whispered. "It's been way too long."

Wait. This woman knew her? Debbie's curiosity got the best of her. She took in the woman's face—and recognized it.

Her stomach knotted, and she closed her eyes. *Oh, Lord. I'm really not ready for this.*

But would she ever be ready to face Sara Loring?

As Greg was wrapping up his talk, one of the girls jumped out of her chair. "A meteor!"

"Good eye." Greg gave her a thumbs-up. "We should see them fairly consistently from here on, but the best display will be right before dawn. So some of you might want to go to bed now and get up before the sun. If we're out here before five, we should get a good show. First light is around six."

Ashling thanked Greg, and the whole group applauded. "You all have your cabin assignments," Ashling said, "but anyone who wants to sleep out on the ground all night is more than welcome to."

Debbie pulled out her phone and checked for messages. She told herself Madeline or Diana might have tried to contact her while her ringer was silenced. That was a possibility, but in truth she was buying a moment of time to gather her thoughts before turning to Sara and—what? Apologizing? Pretending she'd forgotten all about everything that had happened the last time they'd seen each other?

With a deep breath, she stood, slid her phone in her pocket, and turned to face…an empty chair. Sara was gone.

She breathed a sigh. *I will speak to her, Lord. I just need a little more time.*

"You there! Whose cockamamie idea was it to tell a bunch of teenagers they could sleep on the ground all night in the middle of the wilderness?" Nomi strode toward her on short but powerful legs, narrowed eyes lasered on Debbie. "The email said nothing about sleeping out-of-doors. It said we would be sleeping in cabins. Now my girls have it in their heads they're going to be blissfully snoozing under the stars. Do you have any idea how many deadly species are lurking in these woods? Copperheads, rattlers, black widows, brown recluse, coyotes, ticks! I'll not have my granddaughters exposed to Lyme disease because some irresponsible adults—"

"Hello, Mrs. Fairchild. I'm so glad you brought the girls." Keeping her tone pleasant, Debbie gestured to the firepit, where Macy and Morgan sat in lawn chairs on either side of Suki. "Suki's new here too. I suppose the girls told you she's a foreign exchange student. She's been getting teased by some of her host sister's friends. It's making her anxious about school starting. I'm so glad she and your granddaughters seem to be hitting it off."

"Yes, well, she won't find better friends than my son's girls. But you're not going to sidetrack me so easily. This is a dangerous, foolhardy expedition."

Expedition? Debbie couldn't help but picture Ashling as Ernest Shackleton, leading them to Antarctica via the creek that wound through the little valley. Their ship trapped and finally crushed by ice. Subsisting on seals and penguins instead of hot dogs and s'mores. It took all her willpower not to snicker at the idea.

"My girls are not prepared for this. They have never slept outdoors."

"Sleeping under the stars is entirely optional, Mrs. Fairchild. I would imagine most people will be opting for a nice, cozy cabin. And for those who do choose to sleep out here, Ashling has an abundance of bug spray available."

"What about bear spray?"

It took monumental determination not to laugh. She did, in fact, have pepper spray hanging from a clip on her backpack. She'd bought it for dogs, but it would work for bears. If there were any. "Yes, we have that too." She let out a breath as Greg approached. "You remember Greg Connor from the meeting."

Greg took Nomi's hand in his. "Nice to see you again, Mrs. Fairchild. I'm an avid follower of your Gastro Gnome blog."

Did a week's following count as "avid"? And didn't that word imply something positive?

Nomi actually smiled. Even her hard shell was not immune to Greg's charming manner.

"As the president of the chamber of commerce, I would like to extend you an official welcome to Dennison, Ohio, 'a great place to call home.'"

"So I've heard." The tight-lipped expression returned. "Maybe you're the person I need to talk to about the parking in front of…"

Greg subtly patted Debbie's arm, a silent communication that he could take it from there. Debbie grasped his hand in gratitude then nodded to Nomi and stepped away to find Ashling.

Instead, Janet found her. She held a plastic container with a clear lid. "I saw you chatting with Sara. Is this the first time you've seen her since you moved back?"

First time since I was fourteen. "Yes."

"It's such an uplifting story, isn't it? How she came here again years after what those awful girls did to her. Gives a person hope, doesn't it?"

"Uh-huh." It was all she could squeeze out through a tight throat. *Awful girls.* Janet didn't know she was one of them. She'd always been too ashamed to admit it. After a few calming breaths, she asked, "Did she leave already?"

"Yes. She said she was hoping to talk to you more. I guess Nomi got to you first." Janet grimaced. "She wanted to stop by and make sure we didn't need anything. And she left these for you. She remembered that you used to like them."

Snickerdoodle cookies. Sara had brought them with her to camp. How, after all that had happened to her here, could she have remembered that Debbie loved snickerdoodles?

"That was nice of her." Unbidden, more words from the twelfth chapter of Romans came to mind. *Do not repay anyone evil for evil. Be careful to do what is right in the eyes of everyone. If it is possible, as far as it depends on you, live at peace with everyone. Do not take revenge, my dear friends, but leave room for God's wrath, for it is written: "It is mine to avenge; I will repay," says the Lord. On the contrary: "If your enemy is hungry, feed him; if he is thirsty, give him something to drink. In doing this, you will heap burning coals on his head."*

For years, she'd tried to live by those words. Never, as far as she knew, had she ever been on the receiving end of that kind of undeserved grace.

She ran her hand through her hair. She'd never fully understood the part about the burning coals. Until now.

Dennison, Ohio
June 6, 1942

Roxy, Caroline, Minnie, and Jade sat in a close circle in the shade between two cabins. It was too hot to be inside. Since this was the first time Minnie and Caroline had met Jade, there were many whispered questions. "How did you get here?" "Were you scared?" "Have you heard from your parents at all?"

As Jade told them about her encounters with several people on the train, she had them all laughing as quietly as possible. "There was a little boy who said I looked like a bug with such big glasses, and a sweet little old lady who asked if I had a headache. She said she always wore dark glasses when she had a migraine, so I nodded, and then she went to the dining car and brought me some ice in a cloth. She was so kind I almost cried."

The laughter they'd shared a moment ago evaporated, and three of them sat in somber silence as Jade explained the painful choice she and her parents had made. The girls clustered close to her as she told them about saying goodbye to her parents the night before they were to be transported.

"You left all your things in your house?" Caroline asked.

Jade shrugged. "Since I had to take the typewriter and paper, I couldn't bring much else."

"Good thing we wear the same size." Roxy tried to cheer her, but the sadness on Jade's face didn't change until the sound of an axe striking wood caused her face to twist into a mask of fear.

"What was that?" Minnie asked, her expression reflecting the same emotion.

"That's what we need to find out." Jade pulled a stack of folded papers from her back pocket. "There are men, at least three of them, working down by the barn in the valley."

"Farmers?" Caroline asked.

"Maybe. But I don't think so. I climbed up to the top of the hill Roxy said is called Jupiter's Helm."

"The one above the cave?" Minnie asked.

"That's the one. I've watched them a couple of times, but I couldn't tell what they were doing. There always seems to be one man posted near the camp entrance."

"Posted? Like a guard?" Roxy asked.

"Yes. That makes me think what they're doing might not be legal. And that's why I need your help."

CHAPTER EIGHTEEN

Debbie yawned and hugged her hoodie closer to her body as she and Suki tiptoed out of Cabin Three shortly after four thirty on Sunday morning. The sky was still dark peppered with points of light, like a swath of velvet scattered with diamonds. As she stepped off the bottom step, two streaks of light shot across the sky.

Suki settled cross-legged on a blanket occupied by two other girls, who welcomed her with drowsy smiles. Debbie's camp chair sat next to Greg. Though upright, he was encased to his neck in a thin sleeping bag. The shadow on his unshaven face was accentuated by a soft red glow—embers drifting up from the campfire as one of the girls stirred it with a long fork.

Burning coals. She'd gone to sleep thinking about them. Her initial response to Nomi had been to step back and defend herself. Had Sara approached her in Nomi's confrontational manor, she would have put up her guard. Instead, Sara had greeted her like an old friend, cookies and all. No better way to disarm those who persecute you.

Lord, forgive me for not talking to her. It appeared Sara had already forgiven her, but the next chance Debbie got, she would apologize anyway, on behalf of the insecure girl she once was, who had found out the hard way that there was more to life than being one of the cool kids. Maybe she would even thank Sara for the lesson.

As she settled into her chair, a hand slid over hers. "Get any sleep?" Greg's groggy voice asked.

"Probably more than you. Have you been awake this whole time?"

"Awake and fighting off mosquitoes." He pointed to a chair on the other side of the firepit where Ashling slept under a sheet, knees pulled to her chest. Next to her, Tiffany was curled in an almost identical position. Three sleeping bags lay on the ground next to them, a tangle of hair spilling from the top of each one. "Gotta admire them. They toughed it out all night."

"Gotta admire you too." She nudged him, and he grinned. "I feel like such a wimp." She'd let Suki decide where she wanted to sleep and was secretly grateful she'd chosen a bunk in the cabin over a sleeping bag on the hard ground, though she could have tolerated a night of chatting with Greg under the stars. She was also thankful her cabinmates—Suki, Macy, Morgan, and Nomi—had not been chatty last night. She'd dreaded spending that time with Nomi, but peace and quiet had reigned after they all crawled into bunks.

Tipping her head back, she stared up at the sparkling points of light in the dark expanse above them.

Greg leaned close. "Wishing on a star?"

She nodded. She hadn't formed it into words as a wish, but it had been the prayer silently running in the background for weeks.

He squeezed her hand, letting her know he'd guessed what it was.

A tiny light came on beneath the sheet over Ashling. She fought her way out of her cocoon and tapped her watch to shut off the light, and probably the vibration. "Mornin'. Sort of." She seemed to remember why she'd been awakened before the sun and tilted her head up.

Half a dozen streaks of light scraped across the night sky. "Wow." The word came out on a sigh.

She nudged the sleeping form next to her, and Tiffany emerged like a groggy butterfly. Ashling woke the girls on the ground, who sat up blinking then gazed in awe at the light show overhead.

In minutes, nearly everyone had joined the circle.

"We sometimes refer to meteors as shooting or falling stars," Greg said. "The trails of light are streams of cosmic debris called meteoroids entering Earth's atmosphere at extremely high speeds and becoming incandescent as a result of friction."

"Sometimes they hit the earth and make huge craters, right?" asked a girl who would be a freshman this year. She had to be thirteen or fourteen, but she appeared younger. The question was asked with a mixture of wonder and fear.

"Actually, every single day the earth is bombarded with literal tons of debris from space."

The girl sat up straight, eyes wide.

Greg grinned. "But a lot of it is so small that it's hard to see with the naked eye. Think the size of dust or grains of sand. And it often falls into the ocean."

The girl smiled, her relief obvious.

"But about once a year, an asteroid the size of a car enters our atmosphere, creating a massive fireball." He paused for dramatic effect, clearly enjoying the open-mouthed expressions around him. "And then burns up before reaching the Earth's surface."

Several of the girls exhaled loudly. For the next few minutes they sat in silence, broken only by murmurs of appreciation as they watched the heavens.

Around five, the muffled sound of a phone alarm broke the silence. Moments later, Morgan and Macy exited the cabin like identical sleepwalkers. Macy had both hands in the pocket of her hoodie. Morgan appeared to be hiding something behind her back. Instead of heading straight to the teen section in the circle, they stopped next to Debbie, and Suki came to join them.

Macy grimaced. "You won't be mad at us if we tell you something, will you?" she whispered to Debbie.

"And you won't tell Grandma, will you?" Morgan's voice was equally low.

"I can't make promises until I know what you did."

The three exchanged glances and seemed to come to an unspoken agreement.

Macy drew in a long breath. "Well, we have to tell you because this is way too awesome."

"Last night," Suki said, "after you were asleep, we snuck out."

And she hadn't heard them? Apparently she wasn't the only one. Debbie raised an eyebrow at the man who'd said he'd spent the night fighting off mosquitoes.

Greg shrugged. "I must have dozed for a minute or two."

Debbie swiveled in her chair to make eye contact with Suki. "So you snuck out. And?"

"We went exploring in the woods," Morgan said.

"And we found this. It was covered in vines." Macy pulled her phone out and showed the screen to Greg and Debbie.

It was a photo of a rickety-looking wooden shed. The half-moon cutout on the door told her what it was. "You found an outhouse." An interesting find but not worthy of the shimmer in the girls' eyes.

"Macy and Suki dared me to go inside, so I did." Morgan wrinkled her nose at her sister. "And I found this on the inside of the door."

Debbie expected to see another photo, but instead, Macy held out a board. A board with a half-moon cutout. "The door was falling apart. This was the top board." She handed it to Debbie. "Look on the back."

Two carved symbols. The first was shaped like a tent or maybe a Japanese temple. The figure next to it resembled a ladder with legs curved to the left. The symbols were followed by a series of vertical lines about an inch high. "Suki?"

"It says 'June.' We think the lines are for the days Jade was out here."

Debbie stared at the markings. Was this another puzzle piece? Was it possible they'd found something written by Jade? "The latrine and shower houses are on the original blueprint for the camp. They would likely have been built and functioning by the time the camp opened in 1947. So why an outhouse?"

"This might have been built for the construction workers," Greg said.

Debbie ran her fingertip along the row of marks, slowly counting under her breath. "Twenty-nine. If you're right about this, she was here nearly a whole month." Debbie couldn't imagine roughing it that long.

"But that's not the important part. This one was right under it." Macy held out a second board. Morgan aimed her flashlight at it so they could see.

More letters. These in English and scratched in, not carved nearly as deep as the other markings.

Morgan moved her flashlight slowly from left to right, lighting up the words. It took Debbie a few seconds to be sure she was reading it right.

STAY AWAY. OR ELSE.

The smell of bacon frying on the cast-iron griddle set over the firepit drew yawning kids out of sleeping bags and sleepy adults from cabins. Ashling had enlisted the girls who hadn't gone back to bed at sunup to help with breakfast. The twins flipped bacon while Suki cracked eggs. Janet had brought a selection of muffins, and Greg served campfire coffee from a chipped white enamel pot that might have been in his family for generations.

Debbie filled disposable cups with orange juice, then held out a platter as Macy lifted perfectly crisped bacon from the griddle. When the food was arranged on a folding table, Ashling invited a girl named Christina to say grace. She offered up a simple but heartfelt prayer of blessing.

After breakfast, Ashling had the girls count off and then divided them into teams of three. Tiffany gave each of them three index cards—each set containing drawings of a plant, a bird, and a small animal—and a map of the camp. Then she explained that they would work in teams for a scavenger hunt. "The first team to return with pictures or samples of all three things wins."

"You have ten minutes to get ready, and then I'll start a timer for one hour," Ashling directed. "I have prizes for the teams that come in first, second, and third place."

The girls dashed away, laughing and chattering excitedly.

Debbie turned to Janet, Ian, and Greg. "Anyone feel like a hike to an abandoned barn?"

Pants tucked into socks, coated with insect repellant, and armed with water bottles, they walked along the ridge behind Maple Bluff until Ian spotted what had once been a path. "The first couple yards are kind of steep, but it levels out after that." He took a step down and offered his hand to Janet. Greg followed, doing the same for Debbie.

With a walking stick in one hand, she didn't really need his help, but she wasn't about to refuse. Looking down at her hand encased in his, she gave in to a moment of pure gratitude. She'd once thought a long and lasting relationship was not in God's plan for her life.

The overgrown path was flanked by knee-high grass. As they picked their way down the incline, Greg, who was now behind her, muttered. "Watch out for copperheads, rattlers, black widows, brown recluses, coyotes, and ticks."

Debbie slowed. "Were you eavesdropping?"

"I was monitoring. I saw the gnome set her sights on you, and I wasn't about to let her hurt you."

"How chivalrous of you."

"I'm glad you talked her down, though. I wasn't convinced I could have fought her off."

She laughed. "I was using the 'a soft answer turns away wrath' approach. But I wasn't sure it was going to work." She hadn't gotten the twins' permission to share Nomi's story with anyone but Janet, so she'd keep that to herself. But she could comment on her hunches. "I think she's hurting. I'm hoping we can soften her edges a bit."

"If anyone can do that, you can."

She hoped he was right. And once again the thought crossed her mind that she needed to not only apologize to Sara but explain how the shame she'd felt after contributing to her hurt had helped to shape the person she wanted to be today. She had to right the wrongs she had caused.

"I'm glad you're adventurous. Have I ever told you that?" he asked. "You're not afraid of snakes or vicious gnomes. I admire that about you."

She chuckled. "Oh, I'm scared, but the definition of courage is feeling the fear and doing it anyway."

"That makes me even more impressed."

"I think we can cut through here," Ian said.

They were on level ground. That fact surprised Debbie. She'd been so distracted by her conversation with Greg that she'd hardly been aware of the progress they'd made.

The grass was higher here, shoulder-high in places, and there was no path. Debbie had to trust that Ian had a good sense of direction and was leading them the right way.

"We're here," he called moments later.

They caught up with him and stared at a crumbling wall of rocks the size of large watermelons. Debbie felt a sense of reverence for the hands that had built the barn so long ago. Rocks dug up, hauled, and stacked by hand.

Rusted wheels remained in the metal track the barn door had once slid on. Barn doors were popular these days. The farmer who had built this more than a century ago would likely have laughed at the thought of them installed in high-end master suites.

Conscious of Sara's warning about nails and broken glass, Debbie carefully stepped through the opening, startling several pigeons from their perch on a collapsed beam. The flap of wings as they exited seemed to accentuate the desolation.

Half a dozen stanchions remained, partially buried under rotting boards. In one corner Debbie saw a mound of rusted cans with triangular-shaped openings in the top. "When did they start making beer cans out of aluminum?"

"In the late fifties or early sixties, if I'm not mistaken," Greg answered. "I had a college buddy who collected them."

"Seems this was quite the party place some decades ago."

"This is cool." Janet held up an old lantern. The globe was gone, but the rest was intact.

Greg hoisted himself onto one of the stanchions and then onto the top of the wall. He stood, and began walking around the perimeter, stepping over spiked timbers still attached to the wall.

"Be careful," Debbie said without thinking.

He chuckled. "Yes, dear."

Ian lifted a board then pulled out a one-legged stool, the kind a farmer would have hung from his waist by a strap. It would supply enough support to balance on while milking.

They picked their way around in silence for several minutes until Greg stopped and crouched. "I see something." He shifted to hands and knees on the thick wall and bent low, peering into a wide crack once filled with mortar.

"Make sure you can see where you're reaching," Ian warned.

Greg pulled out his phone and aimed the flashlight into the opening. "Uh, Ian? You need to see this."

"What is it?"

"I'm pretty sure it's a gun."

Dennison, Ohio
June 6, 1942

Roxy, Jade, Minnie, and Caroline sat on the floor in the dark in Jade's cabin as the sun, visible through a small gap at the bottom of a boarded-up window opening, sank below the trees.

On the floor in the middle of their circle lay one of the papers Jade had handed out earlier. "The army would call this a reconnaissance mission," Roxy said. "My dad can't ever tell us where he is, but he has written about spying on the enemy to figure out their next move. That's what we did."

"But we still don't know what they loaded on the truck or what they're doing with it," Minnie pointed out.

Nevertheless, their plan had worked. They now knew the men were up to no good. Though they hadn't been able to see inside the barn, observing the men's furtive movements from three different lookout spots had shown that the men were constantly watching their backs, clearly trying to avoid being caught. Whatever they were loading into the truck that was parked halfway in the barn was likely stolen property. "That's why we have to carry out the next phase."

"Next phase?" Caroline's voice quivered. "What is—" A low rumble on the gravel road halted her question.

"They're leaving," Minnie whispered, expressing the relief they all felt.

"Time for the rest of our reconnaissance," Jade said.

"We aren't going down there, are we?" Caroline asked.

"Not if you don't want to. But I'm going."

Caroline took a long, slow breath and squared her shoulders. "Me too."

Roxy and Minnie echoed her response.

Caroline reached behind her and pulled three flashlights from her pack and handed one to Jade and one to Roxy. "My uncle is a police officer. He gave these to my dad."

Minnie took out her own flashlight, but no one turned theirs on. They stood and walked quietly out beneath a moonlit sky streaked with pink.

"Ursa Major and Ursa Minor." Caroline pointed to the eastern sky. "And that's Polaris, or the North Star. Now I can tell my father we identified constellations."

Jade gestured for them to head around the back of the cabin. "We need to be quiet as we get closer, and keep the flashlights off until we know for sure no one is still here."

They made their way downhill through the underbrush. When they stepped into a tangle of raspberry bushes, Roxy wished she hadn't worn shorts. She winced as tiny thorns scraped her calf then felt a trickle of blood seep into her socks.

With its shuttered windows above closed doors, the barn reminded Roxy of a sleeping giant. Jade held out her arm, and they stopped in the tall brush. They waited, watching for light or movement and listening for sound until Jade finally signaled the all clear. They followed her around to the back of the barn, away from where the tire tracks stopped.

"Lights on," Roxy whispered.

They switched their lights on, dispelling some of the dark but creating eerie shadows under the massive oak that hovered over the barn like a clawed hand. When they pointed the lights at the barn, something white was visible between the cracks.

Roxy poked a finger into one of the spaces and touched rough cloth. She pushed, and the fabric gave a bit. It wasn't until she shined her light a little higher that she saw the letters.

She stepped back.

"What is it?" Minnie poked her walking stick through one of the cracks. A stream of white cascaded to the ground, sparkling in the light.

Roxy swallowed hard as she remembered something Mr. Franklin had mentioned. "It's sugar."

CHAPTER NINETEEN

efinitely military issue. Army, probably." Ian held the hand-
gun with the bottom of his T-shirt to avoid compromising
possible fingerprints.

"How old?" Greg asked.

"Forties or older, if I had to guess."

"So it could have been stashed when Jade Tanaka was out here?"

"Could have been."

Debbie stared at the weapon, questions filling her mind. "What
are the chances the police could have missed a bullet hole in the
body found out here in 1942?"

"Unlikely." Ian set the gun on the foundation. "It's more likely
that they found it but covered it up. I've read some old reports from
the forties. There was a police chief in town with some questionable
ethics. He wasn't in office long, but who knows who was greasing
his palms while he was?"

"I bet Cliff Harmon would help us," Janet suggested.

Ian grinned. "That's why I married you." He set the gun on the
rock wall then pulled out his phone.

Debbie had a vague recollection of the man. She'd met him at a
picnic Janet and Ian had hosted. "He was a police officer years ago,
right?"

"He retired soon after I joined the force," Ian said. "But while he was there, he took me under his wing. He could have been a big-city detective instead of a small-town cop, but he loves Dennison and always has. I bet he's solved a dozen cold cases since retiring. Nothing he'd love more than helping solve a new mystery." He held his phone up. "Anyone have a decent signal?"

The other three checked their phones to no avail. Debbie slid her phone in her pocket. "How about we keep searching for a few minutes and then head up? I'd like to be there when the girls get back from their scavenger hunt."

Greg hopped back onto the wall and continued his search of the perimeter. This time, Debbie resisted the temptation to tell him to be careful. She picked up a stick and poked around in the pile of old beer cans. She found a scratched and dented metal bowl. Below that was a bent spoon. She showed the others.

"This would have made a nice hideout for a train hopper back in the day," she observed.

Debbie recalled a book she'd read about a man who'd lost his job as a bank executive when the market crashed in 1929 and ended up doing exactly that, traveling from town to town, looking for work. Hard times created desperate measures.

"Found a quarter." Janet held up the coin. The dull metal still caught the sunlight. She rubbed her thumb across the surface. "1936."

"Denver or San Francisco?" Ian asked.

"What do you mean?"

"Is there a 'D' or an 'S' on it? It'll be on the tails side, right under the olive branches. If there isn't a letter, it was minted in Philadelphia."

"Twenty years of marriage, and now I find out you're a coin expert?"

Ian laughed. "I learn a lot when pawnshops or antique shops are robbed."

Janet squinted at the coin. "There's a 'D.' Does that mean we're rich?"

"It means you might be able to buy me a small coffee."

Janet let out an exaggerated sigh. "But this could have fallen out of the pocket of the killer."

"Or the killed," Greg added.

"Or Roxy or Jade or Minnie." Debbie tried to picture the barn intact. What had it been like in 1942? New and freshly painted, or was it old and weathered even then? Was it still in use? She knew it was part of the camp property, but the Girl Scouts could have rented it out to a local farmer.

Ian started pulling boards off a pile in the corner opposite Debbie. After a minute he held up an old three-prong hay rake. When Greg finished his walk around the wall, he jumped down and helped Ian lift a massive panel of boards still nailed together. They leaned it against the rock wall, and then Ian bent again and lifted what appeared to be a piece of cloth.

Debbie stopped poking around the pile of junk in the corner. "What is it?"

"A bunch of ripped cloth."

"Obviously a mummy was stored here." Debbie laughed when Greg shot her an incredulous look. "Sorry. I've spent too much time with a couple of imaginative boys lately." She dropped her stick and walked over to the men.

"It's a pile of feed sacks." Ian continued to lift the ragged and mildewed pieces one at a time. "No bones. Not human anyway. It was a thriving mouse hotel at one time."

"Wait." Debbie shined her flashlight onto the pile. "There's something written on a couple of them."

Ian fished around until he caught one toward the bottom with pale red and blue letters still visible. He lifted it higher, angled it into direct sunlight, and then flipped it over.

Greg let out a low whistle. "That could easily have been a sugar sack."

Debbie gave a slow nod. "I think you're right. See the logo there?" Though faded, the words were still readable.

Great Lakes Sugar Company

Once again, they all stood in silence for a moment. Debbie recalled what they'd read about the disappearance of four tons of sugar being shipped by rail from the Great Lakes Sugar Company in Paulding, Ohio. "So they, whoever they were, unloaded all of this from the train and brought it here. Then what?"

Ian ran a hand through his hair. "Probably rebagged it in smaller quantities."

"Then distributed it to stores and bakeries, maybe restaurants," Greg added.

Janet used a stick to pick up a bag. "And as far as we know, they were never caught."

"Until now. If we can find out who the gun belonged to, we might crack this case." Ian wrapped the gun in the sugar sack. "Let's head back."

No one argued. They walked up the slope without talking. Debbie could imagine the gears rotating in each head, trying to fit the pieces together.

When they reached the top of the ridge, Ian tapped his phone screen.

"Hey, Cliff. This is Ian Shaw. Got a minute?" He apparently received an enthusiastic affirmative because he laughed then started describing where they'd found the gun. "It's an Army-issue hand-gun circa World War II, but I can't find a serial number. We've seen some evidence that something illegal happened out here in 1942, and we're wondering if the gun could be connected. There was a body found in a shallow grave not far from the tracks that same year. Thinking all those things might be tied together." He listened for a minute then asked, "Mind if I put you on speaker? I'm with Janet and a couple of friends." He tapped the screen again.

"Hello, Janet and friends." The voice was strong, coated with excitement. "I'll tell you what I know. If I'm thinking of the same case, the body was found in a shallow grave, reburied as a John Doe, and then exhumed a few years later, when the guy's wife or mom identified him by a wedding ring. I'm sure I can find more info."

"Any chance they found a bullet in the casket?" Ian asked.

"Not that I remember, but if that was during that Italian gang-ster's reign, who knows? The rest of my day is free." He chuckled. "What am I saying? The rest of my *days* are free. I'll get back to you as soon as I find something. And feel free to bring that weapon over. Slim chance we'd find prints, but you never know."

Debbie stifled a yawn as she walked toward her car after the church picnic. She had exactly two plans for the rest of the day. The first was a nap. After that, she intended to compile everything they'd learned so far about what had transpired at Camp Saundustee in the summer of 1942. Perhaps laying it all out would clarify some connections she'd missed. Plus, she wanted to have the facts at her fingertips if Diana called and she had an opportunity to ask Roxy a few questions. And she wanted to keep a record for the depot. This was a story that needed to be told. Would they ever know all of it?

Ashling appeared beside her with a plastic bowl tucked beneath her arm like a football. "Thanks again for all your help."

"I thought you'd be asleep by now."

"That's next on my agenda."

"You did a wonderful job. We are all so proud of you."

"Thank you." With a yawn followed by a wave, Ashling headed for the parking lot.

"Tired?" a familiar voice asked.

Debbie blinked blearily at Greg. "Exhausted. I can't believe you're still vertical."

"Given the choice of going home and sleeping or coming to see you, I'd give up sleep every time. That said, I'm going home to zonk out for about sixteen hours. You?"

She told him her plans. "If you wake up before nine tonight and want to help me catalog and organize, give me a call."

"I wasn't close enough to eavesdrop when the gnome lady was leaving camp this morning. Everything go okay?"

"More than okay. First she thanked Ashling and said her grand-daughters were excited to be part of her troop. Then, she actually apologized to me and admitted she often missed out on things because she was fearful, and she didn't want to pass that on to her grandchildren."

"She doesn't know her girls sneaked out during the night, right?"

"Pretty sure she doesn't. I wasn't about to be the one to tell her."

"I overheard one of the twins telling Suki it was the biggest adventure they'd ever had."

Debbie touched his arm. "I'm glad you don't keep your boys from having adventures."

Pride glinted in Greg's eyes. "I try."

"You're a good dad. And now, I'm going to go home and—"

Julian sprinted toward them. "Dad, Debbie, I found out something about monkshood."

Greg arched one eyebrow. "What's that?"

"Well, I was talking to Corey, and he asked if monkshood has only ever been used for poison. I hadn't thought about that, so we looked it up on my phone. And apparently, it's also been used as a sedative or local anesthetic, and it has other medicinal purposes as well, as long as you process it first to reduce the poison itself. So maybe the Girl Scouts were really trying to help the poor guy, but they killed him instead because they didn't know they had to make it less dangerous first."

Debbie was pretty sure she mirrored Greg's grimace. "Or maybe the man was trying to ease the pain himself. The report didn't say he was poisoned."

"But what if they couldn't test for that back then?"

"True." She smiled at him. The boy's enthusiasm and impulsiveness might get him in trouble at times, but it was also endearing. "That's helpful information. I might not be quite as quick to blame the Girl Scouts, but I do think you're on the right track. Keep researching."

Once again, she started to say goodbye. This time, she was stalled by Jaxon. He strode up to them, holding out his phone. "I got a text from Suki. Great news."

"What is it?" Julian asked eagerly.

"She went home about half an hour ago, and she'd gotten an email from her grandfather. He found more information about the Tanaka family." He read from his phone. "'A man named Kenji Tanaka translated more than twenty Christian books into Japanese in the forties and fifties.'"

"That's great," Debbie said.

"But here's the cool part. Some of them were translated by Kenji *and* Jade Tanaka, and he found a newspaper article with an interview of Jade when she visited Tokyo in 1972. She said she and her father were indebted to friends in Ohio for helping them continue their work while her parents were confined in Arizona during the war.'"

"Helping how?" They already knew Roxy's mother had sponsored Jade's parents, allowing them to be released from the detention camp. "Did she actually say 'while' her parents were confined?"

Jaxon scanned the text message. "Yep."

"Maybe the Brittons made arrangements somehow so Jade's dad could keep working while he was in that horrible place." It was all she could think of when she was so tired.

"Maybe." Greg rubbed his chin. "After a long nap, I'll do a search for some of those books. We might need Suki to do some translating for us."

Jaxon grinned. "I think we could make that happen."

Squinting at the clock on her nightstand, Debbie yawned and stretched. If it was 4:16, she'd napped for more than two hours. She'd fallen asleep reading Francie's notebook entries. Instead of continuing to page through the notebook in order, she'd skipped to the back. The last thing she remembered reading was a page about things Francie was scheduling for a plant identification badge. Her plans included a hike at "camp" on Saturday, July 10, and she'd listed things each girl was supposed to bring. There were eleven girls on the list. Jade was not one of them.

After arranging three pillows behind her back, she flipped to the middle of the notebook. Two pages in, she stopped at a line that said, *Buy tw paper and ink for J.*

Paper made sense. Jade was likely writing letters to her parents and maybe to friends. But what was "tw"?

"Typewriter!" she exclaimed as it hit her. It had to be. Typewriter paper and ink. But why would she need those things out in a cabin? And why was it ink rather than ribbon?

Had Jade translated books during her stay at Camp Saundustee? But she was translating books from English to Japanese. Would someone in the US have a typewriter that could print the Japanese written language, called *kanji*, in the forties?

She picked up her phone and entered *when Japanese typewriter invented*, then read her findings.

The first Japanese typewriter available to the general public was invented in 1915 by Kyota Sugimoto. There were 2,400 characters on it, chosen from what he had found to be most common in public documents.

The Japanese typewriter was large, heavy, and not user-friendly. Where English-language typewriters allow users to type letters quickly, to write a sentence on a Japanese type-writer, the typist needed to hunt for more than twenty sym-bols among more than 2,000. When selected, the symbol would be run over a small ink wheel before striking the paper. This process was much more time-consuming than the same task on an English machine. Specialized training was required—

Her phone, silenced for her nap, buzzed in her hand, interrupting her reading. She picked up the call. "Hey, Janet."

"Hope you got your rest, girl. Cliff called. We're on a mission."

CHAPTER TWENTY

At five, Greg's truck pulled up, and Debbie waved from the front porch.

Julian jumped out and opened the door for her.

She gave a slight bow. "Thank you, sir."

He grinned at her. "You're welcome, ma'am."

Debbie laughed and got in. She greeted Greg then twisted in her seat to say hi to Jaxon in the back.

"Hi. We're picking up Suki. I thought she could help in case we need anything translated." Jaxon's eyes gleamed. Was she witnessing a bit of a crush? And, she noticed with surprise, he'd given her direct eye contact. Another small step?

"Good idea. What are your guesses? What do you think Cliff found?"

"Has to be a bullet," Julian said. "I bet he found it in an evidence box where they keep all the cold case files. Then we have to shoot the gun Dad found into a block of ballistic gel so we can compare the striations on both bullets. They'll be a perfect match. So we'll get prints off the gun and find out they match Jade's or Roxy's. Then we'll realize they didn't really poison the dead guy. They shot him."

The devious laugh Julian had perfected filled the cab, and the boys high-fived each other.

"You guys have been watching crime scene investigation shows again, haven't you?" Debbie grinned. She enjoyed those shows as much as anyone. "Greg, what's your theory?"

"I'm with the boys—all the way up to identifying the murderer, anyway. I think the guy was shot by the bad cop."

"I like that twist. But why would a police officer hide the gun?"

"He was a dirty cop," Julian said. "He had connections with the mob. He probably had guns hidden all over town."

Debbie went back to staring out the windshield. She didn't want her smile to make Julian think she wasn't taking him seriously. His guess was as good as any, but his air of expertise almost prompted a laugh. "I'm as interested in that officer's story as the rest of our mystery. What makes a small-town cop vulnerable to bribes or extortion? There couldn't have been that much crime going on in little ol' Dennison."

"True," Greg said, "but he may have had connections beyond Dennison. Ian's friend called him the Italian gangster. Lots of history with Italian gangs in Ohio. The Cleveland crime family started in the 1910s and was still going strong in the seventies. Seems at least a possibility the guy could have had that kind of connection. Ah, here we are. The Porters'."

Greg pulled into the driveway of an immaculately landscaped all-brick home. Three swimsuit-clad girls lay on beach towels on the golf course-worthy grass.

"Hi, Jax!" The trio sat up, calling his name in unison.

Jaxon mumbled, "Hi," and walked past them to the front door as Suki came out. When the two passed the group again, one of the girls called out "Goin' to the library with your sweetie, Suki?"

Mindy said nothing, but the arrogant lift of her chin said enough.

As Suki got in the car, Debbie swiveled in her seat. "So good to see you, Suki." Her voice was intentionally louder than it needed to be. "Ready for a fun adventure?"

Suki's expression transformed from tight to delighted. "Yes, I am."

Greg sent Debbie a subtle smile.

Jaxon brought Suki into their speculations about what Cliff might have found until Greg parked behind the Shaws' car at a brick ranch in Uhrichsville.

They walked up to the door, but before Debbie had a chance to ring the bell, the door was opened by a round-faced woman with silver hair. "Come in, come in. I'm Gloria, Cliff's wife. They're all in the family room." She motioned for them to follow her. Over her shoulder she said, "Who would think some old gun could make an eighty-two-year-old man act like an obsessed youngster? He's been on that computer since Ian called. I had to force him to stop and eat lunch."

The comfortably furnished room had obviously been rearranged for this purpose. Round dents in the blue carpeting showed where the love seat and three chairs had recently sat. A folding table took up the middle of the room. Ian, Janet, and a man who must be Cliff stood around it.

Ian made introductions between the newcomers and Cliff, who welcomed them. Turning to Debbie, he said, "I think we met eons ago, long before you teamed up with Janet. She's brought over some of the goodies you all sell, but I haven't had the pleasure of eating at the café yet. I had some health issues, but I had bypass surgery a year ago. The wife still treats me like I need to be handled with kid gloves, even though I'm as tough as any twenty-year-old now." He smirked at a loud snort from the kitchen. "Anyway, I suppose you all came to hear what I found out, not to talk about my problems."

"We are curious," Debbie confessed.

Cliff picked up a sheaf of papers. "Creative title on this first one. 'De Luca Denigrated by Dennison Discovery.' I've highlighted the important parts. In January of 1944, Dennison's police chief, Marco De Luca, was arrested after less than a year in office when the FBI uncovered evidence he was involved in black market trading."

"Like sugar?" Janet asked.

Ian nudged her. "Be patient."

She raised an eyebrow at her husband. "Have you not met me or something?"

He laughed and threw up his hands. "Sorry. I don't know what I was thinking."

Cliff continued. "This doesn't say what part De Luca played, but he was connected with a ring of thieves who were involved in hijacking cattle trucks."

"We read about that in my American history class," Jaxon said. "Those who were involved with the meat black market were called meatleggers."

Julian wrinkled his nose. "Sounds gross."

"Was he convicted?" Greg asked.

"Yep. He was turned in by several of his own officers, indicted, and went to prison." Cliff drew their attention to another page. "This one is about the unidentified body."

"This is an FBI file," Ian said. "Where did you get it?"

Cliff grinned. "Inside sources. Don't worry—it's no longer classified."

"Hope you're right. I don't want to lose my job over this."

"No worries, Chief." Cliff studied the paper. "The body was found in a shallow grave about a hundred feet off the railway five miles east of the Dennison station at 10 a.m. on June 16, 1942."

Debbie exchanged a wide-eyed glance with Janet.

"It was buried in Calvary Cemetery then exhumed in 1946 when the wife of a man who had gone missing four years earlier came across a letter giving instructions for holding up two trains, on two separate dates, in Dennison."

"Exhumation wasn't a common thing back then," Ian said. "Still isn't. After several years the body wouldn't have been identifiable. Even cause of death would have been difficult to determine."

"From what I could find, it was the wife, not the authorities, who asked for the body to be exhumed," Cliff said. "In fact, there appeared to have been some pushback from two of the officers who were hired during De Luca's time in office."

"That's interesting," Greg said.

"The records indicate the man was buried with his wedding ring on, but he had no other personal effects other than clothes. No wallet or identification. Listen to this. 'The body was exhumed by city workers and overseen by Police Chief Ronald Tyler. The ring was recovered and positively identified by Mrs. Carol Phelps as belonging to her husband, Bartholomew Phelps, also known as Bald Bart.'"

"What a strange nickname," Debbie said.

Cliff turned to the second page, stapled to the first. "'After exhumation, the remains were examined by a Tuscarawas County medical examiner. Cause of death could not be confirmed, but damage on the femur was consistent with a gunshot wound. If the femoral artery was hit, he could have died pretty quickly."

Janet voiced the question on Debbie's mind. "So who shot him?"

It was after eight when Debbie got home. They'd gone out for burgers and ice cream after leaving Cliff and Gloria's house. Maybe it was the hot fudge making her restless so that her thoughts swirled like storm clouds, whipping from purple flowers to the girls who had taunted Suki.

Debbie paced her kitchen floor, praying for wisdom. She needed to do something to help Suki. But what?

Ashling. Suki was part of her troop now. Was she aware of what the poor girl was dealing with? She picked up her phone, then set it down again. Ashling lived four blocks away, and it was still light out. It would do her good to burn off some steam and calories.

Ten minutes later she knocked on the door of a little gray house with white trim and bright red front door. Colleen, Ashling's grandmother, opened the door and welcomed her with a hug.

"Is Ashling still up? I know she must be exhausted."

"For some inexplicable reason, she's on the treadmill. I'll tell her you're here."

Moments later, Ashling came up from the basement. She wore shorts and a tank top. Her auburn hair, caught up in a high bun, was damp around her face, and she looked worried. "Everything okay?"

"I could ask you the same thing. Is exercising on a Sunday night when you're already wiped out part of your physical therapy regimen?"

Ashling gave a rueful laugh and gestured for Debbie to have a seat on the sofa. The younger woman sat on the other end. "Not physical therapy. This is the emotional kind."

"What's going on?"

"I witnessed something at the picnic today. Two of Mindy's friends were there. I was too far away to hear, but they were clearly mocking Suki. I'm second-guessing my decision to not intervene. But we can talk about that later. You clearly have something on your mind."

"It appears God has given us this burden to share. I came over because of Suki." Debbie told Ashling what she'd observed when they'd picked up Suki at the Porters. "Suki said she'd been looking forward to school starting, but now she's worried."

"You've spent a little more time with her than I have. Do you think we could talk to her together? She might want to work it out herself, but I want her to know she doesn't have to."

"Of course. I considered talking to the Porters, but that might embarrass her. You're showing some good leadership wisdom, Ashling. If you needed confirmation that you're in the right place at the right time, here it is."

"And if I needed confirmation that I was right to ask some wiser women to help, here you are."

Walking home a few minutes later, Debbie's steps felt lighter. A Bible verse she'd alluded to with Ashling came to mind again. *Carry each other's burdens, and in this way you will fulfill the law of Christ.* Sharing her concerns and knowing Suki was surrounded by people who would pray for her, protect her, and help shoulder her burden left Debbie free to return to the questions raised by the things they'd found at the camp, Cliff's research, and Francie's notes.

Diana might be able to answer some of those questions. Would a call be intrusive when her sister was dying? The last thing Debbie wanted to do was interrupt their last days, or hours, together with something they might consider unimportant. Yet Diana had asked her to call if she discovered anything new.

She stepped into her house and stared at the clock on the fireplace mantel. Its ticks counted out a full minute before she decided to make the call.

Diana answered on the third ring. "Debbie, hello. How are things in Dennison? I was actually thinking of calling you."

"All is well here. We have some new information which has led to a lot more questions, but first I want to know how Roxy is."

"Sleeping a lot. Fortunately she still seems comfortable. She's had a few lucid moments, and I'm praying for more."

"My grandmother said some precious things to all of us in her last few days."

"Roxy and I had that same experience with our grandpa. Now, tell me what you've found out, and then I'll tell you my news."

Debbie settled back on pillows and started with the markings the girls had found on the outhouse door.

"So you're thinking Jade was there the whole month of June?"

"That's my guess. But there's more. Someone had scratched the words 'Stay away. Or else' under the markings."

"A threat, maybe to one or more of the girls?"

"It seems likely." She summed up everything they'd found in what remained of the barn. When she got to the gun, she said, "Of course, it wasn't necessarily connected to the theft of the sugar. It might have been there before or put there long after."

"But it could have been the 'or else' from the outhouse message."

"Yes, it could have been."

"Goodness. I wonder if Roxy knew how much danger she was in. If she was. You've certainly given me a lot of questions to ask her if the opportunity arises."

"I might have a few more for you. I found one of Francie Reese's notebooks. I guess you'd call it a planning notebook. In one of her to-do lists, she wrote 'Buy tw paper and ink for J.' We're pretty sure every time she writes 'J,' it stands for Jade, and I think 'tw' is for 'typewriter.'"

"It makes me so sad that we may never know the whole story," Diana said. "And even more frustrating is not knowing why. After all these years, why wouldn't Roxy or Jade talk about it? It's a story their children and grandchildren deserve to know. Unless—goodness, I shouldn't let my thoughts wander like this, but do you think they might have done something they were ashamed of? Hiding Jade might have defied the government ruling, but public opinion has changed drastically since then. My sister would have been heralded as a hero for what she did, and Jade's bravery would have been commended by many. Why keep it a secret?"

"What do you think Roxy meant when you asked her about the boxcar and she said, 'It will all be clear soon'?"

"I wish I knew. My guess is that someone in the family will receive the key to her safe when her will is read. We might have access to her diaries then, but I'm not sure they would tell us much." Diana chuckled. "I have repented of this, but I confess I was still reading Roxy's diaries right up until she left for college, and she was still writing things so vaguely that I never learned much of anything."

"That's one way to make sure you remember your secrets, but no one else knows them," Debbie said.

"Gayle and I were probably fifteen, which meant it must have been a time Roxy was home on break, when we heard a rumor that a boy had proposed to her. It took us hours to find her diary. She'd wrapped it in a towel and stuck it in the corner behind the claw-foot bathtub. All she'd written was, 'Had a memorable walk tonight.' But she'd turned the *O* in memorable into a diamond ring."

"Almost sounds like she was making the hunt fun for you."

"I think you're right. She was always quite the practical joker. Now, back to what you said before I got us off on a rabbit trail. You mentioned paper and ink. The poor girl was out in the woods surviving on her own, and Francie brought her those things?"

"It specifically says 'tw paper and ink.'"

Diana said, "You mentioned 'typewriter'?"

"That was my guess. I assume you know Jade worked with her father on translating books into Japanese."

"Yes. But—oh! Have you read any of Roxy's books?"

"Just one so far, about a girl alone in a redwood forest. I think it's the first in her Emerald series. I assumed it was inspired by what she did for Jade."

"I'm sure it was. There was another one in the same series. It takes place during the Cold War in the sixties. Emerald hauls her father's secret-code typewriter by train from Los Angeles to Chicago. Her father is a spy for the US, and Emerald is running from the

Russian spies who kidnapped him. She needs the typewriter to communicate with the CIA."

"Wow. Do you think Jade's father was actually a secret agent?"

Diana laughed. "No, but Uncle Ken was dedicated to spreading the Lord's message. In later years, he learned Chinese and Korean and helped smuggle Christian literature and Bibles. Since his work started before the war, I suppose it's possible that Jade helped him while she was in Ohio. Were there Japanese typewriters then?"

"Yes, and they used ink wheels and special paper rather than regular paper and ribbons like English typewriters."

"Maybe that was the reason she didn't stay with her parents. What a brave thing for a girl so young to do."

"So what's your news?" Debbie asked.

"I got a call from Roxy's agent. One of Jade's granddaughters is flying here. If you're a praying person, please pray Roxy is still with us so they can see each other."

"I will do that."

"And here's the best part for you. The granddaughter also wants to visit Dennison."

Sore and stiff from sleeping on the floor of the cabin, Roxy slid the straps of her haversack onto her shoulders and faced Jade. "We might not be able to get away again for a couple of days, but Francie said she and James could come out anytime to bring food and such."

"Okay. How should I plan to get in touch with you if I need to?" *Jade asked.*

Roxy's gaze fell on the green book she'd given Jade a week ago. "Write it in code in the handbook and give it to Francie to give to me." *Five years earlier, when Roxy found that her family was moving to Ohio, she and Jade had created several simple codes so they could write to each other without their parents knowing what they were saying. Not that they thought anything bad would happen if their parents did know, but they loved the idea of encoding their communication.*

And now it seemed that would pay off.

"We all promise we won't tell anyone what we saw, right?" *Roxy asked Caroline and Minnie.*

"Right." They chorused.

"Tomorrow I'll try to get the license plate on the truck so we can report it anonymously," Jade said.

"Not until after my mom gets home and you're safe at our house. If we tell the police now, they'll probably search the whole camp." She didn't need to explain why that would be a problem.

"I made something for each of you." Jade walked to the table Roxy had made, then handed them each a small card. On it were several Japanese symbols and three numbers separated by a colon. "It's Matthew 5:44. 'Love your enemies, bless them that curse you, do good to them that hate you, and pray for them which despitefully use you, and persecute you.' My father gave me a card with this verse on it soon after the country of his birth declared war on the country we call home. I have needed that reminder over and over, and I think it is a good one now, when there is likely an enemy right here."

Roxy flipped her card over. Jade had written on the back.

Roxy, this is our mission. J

"My grandfather prays every day for the soldiers who fight against our soldiers," Minnie said. "I have tried. It's so hard." She glanced at Jade. "I can't imagine how you must feel."

"I would never have thought to pray for those men." Caroline nodded toward the boarded-up window, her expression showing her distaste for the idea.

Roxy kept her thoughts to herself, but she agreed with what she was sure Caroline was thinking. How could she, in all sincerity, pray for people whose goal was to kill men like her father, or for those who intended to make money by stealing food for their own profit?

They said their goodbyes and headed home. So many thoughts swirled in Roxy's mind, filling her with dread and confusion as she rode.

They should report what they knew to the police. Several of the Dennison police officers were her father's close friends. She thought of them as uncles and had always trusted them, but there were others her parents had no respect for, including the chief of police. If she talked to the ones she could trust, what would they do if they found a runaway girl who was supposed to be incarcerated in a detention camp in Arizona? And which was worse—the police who might find Jade, or the men at the camp being allowed to operate for another couple of weeks?

Those thoughts followed her all the way to the Davises' and through the first half hour of church.

It wasn't until Pastor Gerhard read a passage from Matthew that her wild thoughts came to a sudden halt. "Many of us would like to pretend the fifth chapter of Matthew isn't there right now. Keep in mind, these are the words of our Lord Jesus, spoken at a time when He knew what was going to befall Him: 'Ye have heard that it hath been said, Thou shalt love thy neighbor, and hate thine enemy. But I say unto you, Love your enemies, bless them that curse you, do good to them that hate you, and pray for them which despitefully use you, and persecute you; That ye may be children of your Father which is in heaven: for he maketh his sun to rise on the evil and on the good, and sendeth rain on the just and on the unjust.'"

What were the odds of the Lord bringing her those words twice in one day? Roxy sat up, her full attention on the reverend.

"Hard words to hear, are they not? Though most of us would not admit it out loud, aren't we more comfortable with 'An eye for an eye'? Yet, if Jesus calls us to do the opposite of what comes natural to our sin nature, who are we to argue?"

Who are we to argue? The words played in her head like a skipping record for the rest of the day.

CHAPTER TWENTY-ONE

Shortly after Janet flipped the sign to Closed on Monday afternoon, there was a rap on the door. Debbie opened it, and Kim walked in.

"Well hi, Kim," Janet greeted her. "Here for an afternoon pick-me-up?"

"I know you're closed, but I wouldn't say no to that if you're willing," Kim replied.

"Three iced mochas coming up." Janet bustled behind the counter.

Debbie sank into a chair across from Kim at a table by the window. "You found something? Must be important to bring you in on your day off."

"I found several somethings."

They chatted about the busy day while they waited for Janet. When she set glasses and a plate of brownies on the table, Kim held up the book. "The depot logbook for the first six months of 1942." She opened to a page marked with a sticky note then faced Janet and Debbie. The top third of the book was warped. The pages were rippled, and some of the entries were illegible. "I think this might have gotten water damage in 1945 when there was a fire at the depot."

"I didn't know there was ever a fire here."

"Mom said it started in a trash can. Probably a cigarette. They caught it before it got out of hand, but some records were destroyed."

Debbie ran a finger across the bumpy paper, imagining the commotion a fire in the train station must have caused.

The closely spaced rows and narrow columns on the yellowed pages provided blanks for arrival and departure times, the names of conductors and enginemen, the number of cars on the train and its total weight, and a place for remarks. The log was as tidy and thorough as anyone could have wanted.

"There was, indeed, a 5:22 freight train scheduled on June 15, 1942," Kim said, pointing to a line halfway down the page, where a line had been crossed out. "But it seems to have been rescheduled and actually arrived at 6:18 that day." She pointed to the *Remarks* column, where a note said *Loaded McGarry Furniture Factory pallet for Camp Ritchie.*

Camp Ritchie. Where had Debbie read that name? "Camp Ritchie is where the sugar that was stolen off the train on May 31 was headed."

Kim nodded. "I figured that if the pallet from McGarry was headed to a military base in Cascade, Maryland, it stood to reason that other things on that train could have been too. Things that could bring a pretty penny on the black market. So I contacted a local historical society." Kim drummed her fingers on the table. "After the sugar was stolen from a boxcar right here in Dennison on May 31, 1942, the Great Lakes Sugar Company sent another shipment with two armed guards on June 15. It was likely on the freight train that was rescheduled and arrived here an hour late."

"So that's the one the girls found out about," Janet said.

"I think so. I understand the demand for beef or gasoline during rationing, but it's hard to believe people were willing to pay so much for sugar that crooks would risk their lives to steal it."

"Spoken like someone whose business doesn't depend on it." Janet picked up the plate of brownies, passed it under Kim's nose, and then held it out of reach.

Kim laughed. "Okay. I get it. That was very insensitive of me."

"You are forgiven." Janet returned the plate, and Kim snatched a brownie.

Debbie absently listened to the banter as she researched on her phone. "Sugar was selling for eight cents a pound in 1942. Eight thousand pounds would be around six hundred dollars. Doesn't sound like much, but considering the average income was $1,885 a year or about $36 a week—well, that makes it seem like a lot more. It's the equivalent of about $11,000 today."

"And considering that there were businesses that would go under if they couldn't purchase enough sugar," Kim said with a smile at Janet, "the black-market price was probably drastically inflated. Sounds like enough of a motive to hijack a boxcar to me."

Janet bit into a brownie and chewed slowly. "Let's reconstruct this. Somehow, two weeks after four tons of sugar were stolen from a boxcar here at the depot, the girls found out some men were going to stop the 5:22 train on June 15, probably to hijack another sugar shipment. So did their actions save the sugar?"

"The guy I talked to at the historical society didn't have any idea what happened to the train."

"Since it was headed to Camp Ritchie, maybe that's a military question," Debbie said. "I know someone who might be able to help us. His name is Nathan Wade, and he was one of Reed's best friends. He served three tours in Afghanistan and is now a policy analyst at the Pentagon. I'll call him tonight."

More than once, Debbie had told Harry she could set her watch by his arrival, so when she hadn't seen him by eight o'clock on Tuesday morning, she was worried. She was about to call him when the bell above the door tinkled and Harry shuffled in, followed by Crosby, Patricia—and Minnie.

Debbie rushed to greet them. "Minnie, I don't know if you remember me. I'm—"

"Debbie Albright." Her voice quivered a bit, but her gaze was clear and steady. "I used to volunteer at Good Shepherd when you were a little girl. I remember you coming in and reading to the residents when you were a just a tyke."

"That's how I knew you. I remembered meeting a lady named Minnie who loved to sing old hymns."

Minnie's laugh was deep and husky. "That was me. I still love to sing, but only when I'm alone with Jesus now. Wouldn't do that to anyone else."

Harry and Patricia had already settled at their usual table with Crosby under their feet. Debbie pulled out a chair for Minnie. "I'm glad you're feeling better."

"Well, you helped that along, my dear."

"I did?"

"Yes indeed. When Harry called and told me you'd found some interesting things in that old scout book, it brought back so many memories."

Debbie felt her pulse kick up a notch. "Let me take your order, and then we can talk. Janet made cherry turnovers this morning."

Patricia groaned. "That woman is to blame for half my wardrobe not fitting anymore."

Debbie laughed. "You and me both."

"We'll each have one and take three to go," Patricia said. "And Minnie wants to try the peppermint mocha. Cold."

"Coming right up." Debbie filled cups with crushed ice, then asked Paulette and Janet, "Can you two handle things without me for a bit?"

"As long as you take good notes." Janet held two plates in one hand and one in the other. "I'll deliver these. I want to say hi to Minnie."

When the three had their order, Debbie asked if she could join them for a few minutes.

"Of course," Minnie answered at once. "Now, tell me what was in the book."

"First, can I ask why you had it?"

"Did you know Francie Reese?"

"Only from things I've read recently."

"Some years ago, I helped her daughter move her into a memory care facility in Cleveland. She had an entire file cabinet dedicated to her years as a Girl Scout leader and director of Camp Saundustee. She told me to take whatever I wanted. I threw it all in a box, which then sat on a shelf in my closet, made a couple of moves with me, and was finally donated for Kim's Girl Scout display over at the museum. I never opened the book. I had no idea it was Roxy's, or I would have. We haven't corresponded in years. Do you know if she's still alive?"

"She is. I've been talking to her sister. Sadly, it sounds like she doesn't have long."

"Hardest thing about reaching this age, isn't it, Harry?"

"At this point, I've lost too many friends to count," he replied sadly.

Minnie patted his hand. "I'm grateful we still have each other."

"What about Caroline Davis?" Debbie asked. "I haven't been able to find out anything about her."

"Her parents divorced right after we graduated from high school. She moved to Cincinnati with her mother, changed her name to distance herself from her father, became a teacher in one of the roughest neighborhoods, and later joined the civil rights movement. Sadly, she passed in her sixties, but she accomplished a great deal in her life." Minnie smiled. "So what was in the book?"

Debbie had repeated the list so many times in the past two weeks, it didn't take her long to rattle it off, saving the most interesting for last.

"Monkshood? That's highly poisonous!" Minnie's dark eyes were wide. "Why would she put it in a book?"

"We wondered the same thing. Can you tell me what you remember about Jade Tanaka?"

Minnie gaped at Debbie for a long moment. "Who told you about her?"

"The Girl Scout book led us to her. It's been an interesting journey. But there's still so much we hope to uncover. We know Jade's parents were confined in Arizona, Jade herself stayed at Camp Saundustee in 1942, and that you, Roxy, Caroline, and Francie spent time with her out there."

Minnie's shoulders lowered. "All right then. We all pledged not to tell, and I've kept that promise. I've never told anyone about that time. Not even my husband or children."

"Please don't feel pressured. I wouldn't want you to feel you've compromised your integrity. To be honest, we haven't learned much from Roxy. She was awake and alert a few days ago but wouldn't give her sister very straightforward answers. She did say we would find out more soon. Diana didn't know what that meant."

Minnie's eyes sparkled. "Roxy was a storyteller. She loved keeping people in suspense. Years ago, she wrote to all of us, asking if she could write about that summer. We all agreed. If you read her books, you'll see glimpses of the things we did. Some of them, anyway."

"Do you know anything about a train robbery at the depot?"

"The sugar." Minnie stared off into the distance, as if watching a scene from long ago play out in her mind. "So many bags of sugar. Hundreds of dollars' worth."

"In the barn?"

"Yes." Fear, or maybe regret, crossed her face. She closed her eyes for a moment. "There were things we never told Roxy or Jade."

"We?"

"Caroline and I." She picked at a fingernail, apparently trying to decide if she should keep talking. "Roxy could be bossy at times.

Caroline and I wanted to take some of the sugar, but Roxy told us not to. So one day we put some canning jars in a burlap bag and rode our bikes out to camp. I remember being terrified because the three men who'd stolen the sugar were out there cutting down trees, and we were scared we'd get caught."

"Why were they cutting down trees?" Patricia asked. "Sorry to interrupt. I just find that curious."

"I assumed they were shipping them somewhere because they were dragging them to a spot near the tracks. Anyway, we snuck in the barn and cut open one of the bags. We filled our jars, but when we were running to our bikes, we heard the men arguing. We hid behind a huge tree and watched them. One of them, a bald man, said they had to get rid of the girl."

Debbie leaned forward. "Jade?"

"I'm not sure, but I don't know who else it could have been. The other guy—he was a lot younger but looked much stronger—said no. He said she was a kid and he'd given her a warning to stay away, but they weren't going to have murder on their hands. The third guy, skinny and tall, backed him up. All three got into a huge fight, and then the bald guy pulled out a gun. The young guy lunged for it, and in the struggle it went off."

Debbie stared at her. Of all the things she had thought Minnie might say, that hadn't been one of them.

Minnie took a long, shaky breath. "The bald guy was dead. The two others dragged him off, and we followed at a distance. They dug a hole, not very deep, and threw him in. Like he was nothing. I mean, he obviously hadn't been a very nice person, but no one deserves to be treated like that. It was awful. The skinny man said they should say something over the body, but the other man said they didn't have time. He said they'd do that and put some flowers on his grave after they finished the job."

Harry covered her hand with his.

Her dark eyes shimmered. "I never told anyone."

Sometime after Harry, Patricia, and Minnie left the café, Debbie's phone buzzed in her apron pocket. She didn't usually answer during busy times, but she couldn't ignore the feeling that this one was important. Her breath hitched when she saw the name on her screen. "Hi, Madeline," she said softly as she walked into the kitchen.

"Debbie." Her voice was rough. Before she said the words, Debbie knew.

"Diana asked me to call you. Roxy passed away early this morning. She was surrounded by her family, her agent, and one of Jade's granddaughters."

"I'm so sorry. Thank you for letting me know." Debbie felt the loss in her chest. A woman she'd never met was gone, leaving so many mysteries unsolved.

"There will be a memorial service in a couple of weeks. The details are still being worked out. Diana said she'd call you soon. It sounds like she might have some answers to your questions."

"Please tell her not to even think about that now. None of that is important in light of what she's dealing with. And please let her know we're all praying for her."

"Thank you, Debbie. I'll tell her."

The sadness followed Debbie into the afternoon but eased a bit as she reflected on what a remarkable life Roxy had lived. She had witnessed almost a century, long enough to see two countries once at war become allies. She'd fallen in love, had children, been loved by grandchildren. She'd written more than twenty books for young adults. The impact of her words on young lives was immeasurable. A life well lived.

Debbie was on her way home from work when Diana called. After expressing her condolences, she repeated what she'd said to Madeline. "We can talk after Roxy's memorial service."

"Actually, I have something very time-sensitive to talk to you about." The smile in Diana's voice was unexpected. "About an hour ago, Roxy's agent, Jade's granddaughter, and my great-niece, Roxy's granddaughter, purchased plane tickets to Akron, Ohio. They are beginning a tour of the country, and they're going to start in your town. They'll be in Dennison on Thursday afternoon."

"*This* Thursday?" As soon as she said the words, she realized her reaction could be misconstrued. "That's wonderful. I was simply surprised."

Diana laughed. "I know it seems abrupt. It did to me too. But they're carrying out a plan Roxy devised months ago. She wanted them to visit Camp Saundustee after she was gone. They've been on standby, so to speak. I guess that sounds morbid, but the feeling around here is anything but."

"Really?" Debbie asked, amazed.

"Truly. Minutes after my sister took her last breath, Carmen, her agent, whispered, 'Joy comes in the morning.' Suddenly, our tears turned to tears of joy, and we were laughing and joking about what Roxy's first words to Jade would be on their reunion. Roxy lived a full and beautiful life and died peacefully. We will miss her, but the grieving is for ourselves, not her. Now it's time to honor her by carrying out her wishes."

"Is there anything I can do to help? Where are they staying?"

"They're renting a car at the airport, and they have hotel reservations in New Philadelphia. Carmen has already made arrangements with a couple of people they want to meet. You were next on her list. Roxy told them about the Girl Scout book. They can't wait to see it. If you're available, that is."

"Of course. If there's anything else I can do, say the word."

"If you have the time and you'd be interested, I'm sure they'd love a tour guide."

"I would be honored."

Dennison, Ohio
June 15, 1942

Roxy paced the bedroom floor, glancing at her watch every few minutes. Days had passed since they'd seen Jade. Francie had gone out to the camp multiple times and reported that Jade was fine and using the solitude to work, but her words weren't enough to calm Roxy's nerves. And now she had even more reason to pace the bedroom floor.

Yesterday afternoon Francie and James had come to the Davises'. Acting as if they were out for a Sunday stroll, they'd even stayed and visited with Caroline's parents for almost an hour. And then, on their way to the door, Francie had handed her the Girl Scout handbook with no explanation.

As soon as they left, she'd dashed upstairs and found the place where the code started and had flipped through the pages, copying down numbers and letters. It didn't make sense—until she read it backward.

Men watching. Planning stop 522 train. Call police. Meet helm 500 on 615.

Men watching. Watching Jade? The thought made her stomach knot.

There was a 5:22 train today and Wednesday. This morning, when Mrs. Davis had gone next door for coffee with the neighbor, Roxy had slipped out and called the police to report what Jade had written. She'd left it anonymously. Would they take her seriously, especially when she didn't know which day the men were planning to act? Would they have officers at the depot, ready to protect the train when it pulled in?

She glanced at her watch for the hundredth time. 4:27. It would take twenty-five minutes to ride to the camp. If she didn't get caught, she could be there in plenty of time to stand with Jade on top of Jupiter's Helm and watch the 5:22 train pass. If the police were able to stop the hijacking. How far did the sound of gunshots travel? Would they hear them if there was a confrontation?

She glanced out the side window. Diana played hopscotch in the driveway with Gayle and Madeline. She stepped to the bedroom door, listening. Caroline and her mother discussed dinner plans in the kitchen. She hadn't told Caroline what she was doing. No point in both of them getting punished. And she would be punished for sure. When Mr. Davis got home from work at half past five, she would be gone.

After putting on her rucksack, she eased open the window facing the backyard. From there, she would *jump onto the roof of the porch then drop to the grass. If she didn't make a sound or break a bone, she'd be free.*

Her feet skittered on the hot shingles, sending a cascade of black particles onto the grass. Thankfully, they made no sound. Air whooshed from her lungs when she hit the ground, but she wasn't hurt. She ran across the lawn and grabbed her bicycle from behind the garage. Then she was off, riding faster than she ever had before, a mixture of fear and thrill coursing through her.

She and Jade might have prevented the theft of more sugar, or something even more valuable. Her tip might lead to the arrest of the men who were watching Jade.

Or they might have accomplished nothing, might even have sent the wrong authorities out to the camp. Ones who could be in cahoots with the thieves, or even find Jade and send her to prison for the duration of the war.

"Lord, please," she whispered, unsure how to put all her fears into words. Her short prayer wafted away on the wind.

Avoiding the gravel road that led into the path, she hid her bike in a copse of trees then ran along the stream.

As she approached the cave, the sight that greeted her was one of astounding beauty. A sea of purple flowers swayed in the breeze. She'd learned the word incongruous *last year. It was a way to describe a thing not in harmony with something else. Something like danger. The blossoms' color took her breath away. But she'd studied these for her Wild Plant Finder badge. These were blooms that could literally take your breath away.* Beauty and evil living side by side...

Jade waited inside the entrance. Roxy hugged her then studied her friend's face. "You look terrified."

"I am. We can't get back to town in time."

"In time for what?"

"Come with me."

Roxy followed her through a tangle of underbrush to the railroad tracks. When they broke through the trees, Roxy came to a sudden stop. Her stomach lurched.

A pile of massive cut logs blocked the tracks.

CHAPTER TWENTY-TWO

Debbie stood at the window on Thursday after work, watching a car pull up in front of her house. Janet, Ian, and Ashling got out. Moments later, Greg's truck parked behind them. Greg, the boys, and Suki completed the procession heading to her front door. She swung the door open and welcomed them.

The Girl Scout handbook and its contents were spread out on the coffee table, along with a stack of research. Janet brought several framed copies of the photo of Francie and the four girls for their guests, and for Diana, Gayle, and Madeline.

Another car door slammed, followed by two more. As everyone settled in her living room, Debbie went to the door. The three women smiled as they approached. The oldest wheeled a small suitcase. She introduced herself as Carmen St. Laurent, then introduced Hoshi Saito, Jade's granddaughter, and Talia Rivera, Roxy's granddaughter.

After introductions, Janet and Ashling went to the kitchen for coffee and lemonade. Debbie was prepared to make small talk, but Hoshi immediately started asking Suki questions. Where in Japan was she from? What did she think of the US? Apparently, Hoshi had also been a foreign exchange student in the midnineties, spending a whole school year in Los Angeles near where her grandmother had lived at the time. The two immediately connected over comparing their experiences.

When everyone had a beverage, Carmen rested her hand on top of her wheeled case but didn't open it. "In my line of work, I often have occasion to marvel at God's perfect timing. Debbie, the book that led you to Roxy as she was transitioning from this world fits into that category. Hearing how you used the things you found in her book to try to unravel her secrets gave her so much joy in her final lucid moments." She swallowed hard then cleared her throat. "The last thing she said to me was, 'Thank you for taking our story back to its beginning.'"

With a flourish, Carmen unzipped the top flap of the case and pulled out a book.

On the cover was a picture of the cabin Debbie and Suki had slept in five nights before. Across the top were the authors' names—Roxy Britton Keller and Jade Tanaka Saito. On the bottom was the title.

Saundustee Secrets

It took sheer willpower to leave Roxy's book for the weekend. Debbie knew if she started reading on Thursday night, she'd be worthless at the café on Friday. So she waited. After work on Saturday, she and Janet had to make a run to the store to stock up on standard ingredients.

Then, since Ian had to work late, they stopped at a restaurant and shared an order of nachos. By the time Debbie got home and changed into more comfortable clothing, it was after seven. She settled on the couch with a glass of iced tea.

The book began with a letter from Roxy, dated three months before.

> *Dear Reader,*
>
> *Until now, all of my stories have been fiction inspired by reality. Saundustee Secrets is a true story of a summer I will never forget. Why tell this story now, eighty years after it happened? Because I have kept a promise I made to my best friend in June of 1942. Though we penned these pages decades ago, I kept my word that I would not share them until she was gone.*
>
> *At the age of twelve, Jade Aimi Tanaka, in the tradition of her elders and ancestors, made a vow of humility. As the apostle Paul says in the twelfth chapter of Romans in the Bible, it was a vow not to think of herself more highly than she ought, to outdo others in showing honor, to live in harmony with those around her, and not be haughty. She felt that the telling of these events would bring undue attention to herself and not be in keeping with her vow.*
>
> *My dear friend Jade ran into the arms of Jesus in Nagoya, Japan, where she and her husband had served their community for more than forty years. She is free from earth's constraints, and I am now free to tell you of that magical, terrifying, adventurous month she spent at Camp Saundustee.*
>
> *I hope you enjoy your time with us, and I pray you are inspired to do brave things for God.*
>
> *Love,*
>
> *Roxy*

"Love your enemies, bless them that curse you, do good to them that hate you, and pray for them which despitefully use you, and persecute you." Matthew 5:44.

Starting on the next page, the book alternated between Roxy's point of view and Jade's. In the first chapter, Jade described sitting around the radio with her parents and neighbors listening to Lieutenant General John L. DeWitt of the Western Defense Command issue Public Proclamation No. 4, which began the forced evacuation and detention of Japanese-American West Coast residents on a forty-eight-hour notice. Violating the order was punishable by up to one year in prison and a $5,000 fine.

We were stunned. My parents were United States citizens. They had lived in this country for two decades. My sister and I were born here. We were all, from youngest to oldest, in tears. Two months later we received our orders. We had forty-eight hours to pack what we could carry, say goodbye to the friends and neighbors who hadn't already been evacuated to an "assembly center," and move to Arizona.

As Debbie read about the Tanakas' decision to send Jade to her mother's best friend in Ohio, and their heart-wrenching goodbye, she reached for a box of tissues. She wasn't a mother, but she knew how she would have felt in Jade's position—terrified for her parents and wondering whether she would ever see them again, and terrified for herself. All of them heading toward separate unknown fates without the familial support they provided each other.

Around three in the morning, Debbie woke with the book on her chest. She climbed the stairs and fell into bed but couldn't get back to sleep, so she continued to read. By the time she reached the last chapter, sunlight seeped in around the edges of her bedroom blinds, and a pile of damp tissues sat next to her on the bed.

All but a few of the missing pieces had been filled in. Would the last chapter tell her what happened to the 5:22 train?

Vision blurring, she continued to read.

Jade

One morning, I found a message scratched into the inside door of the outhouse. "Stay away. Or else."

Later that day I heard a gunshot.

They had a gun. They knew I was there. I was no longer safe in the cabin.

The men always left the camp around five, so I hid my belongings and decided to spend my days up on the bluff by the cave. From that vantage point, I could watch them. There were only two of them now. The bald man was gone. I couldn't let myself dwell on what might have happened to him, especially after hearing the gunshot.

During the day, I took walks, played in the waterfall, and drew pictures of flora and fauna I saw. Midday, when the sun was hot, I hid in the coolness of the cave. And I watched. Some days the men spent hours in the barn. It didn't take long to realize that they were repackaging sugar in several sizes of paper sacks. They would load crates of sacks into their truck, and then the tall, thin one would drive off and be gone for hours. When he returned, the crates were empty.

Other days, they would fell trees. I thought they were going to build another building or maybe sell the wood.

Each day, when the men left, I went back to the cabin and worked by the light of a kerosene lamp until I couldn't keep my eyes open.

This pattern lasted a few days. One day, the men didn't leave at five. They were still there at sunset. I crept down the hill, scared but determined to find out what they were doing. To this day, I can still feel the adrenaline rush of sneaking around the corner of the barn and crouching under a broken window, trying to slow my heartbeat as I listened.

"Marco said if we pull this off, he's got a bigger job for us over in Columbus."

Debbie stopped reading. Marco had to be Marco De Luca, the police chief Cliff had said was convicted for black market trading. She read on.

"I say we forget Marco," the other voice replied. "You and me can find jobs on our own after this. We got a deal with him for this one. We stop the 5:22, but after that we move on. He ripped us off with the last sugar shipment. He's using us, takin' the biggest cut for himself when we're the ones doin' the work. You stay if you wanna keep doin' his bidding, but I'm not sticking around to be pushed around

anymore. Soon as we're done here, I'm givin' Bart a proper kind of funeral. Wasn't my fault, you know? He asked for it. Still, a man oughta have a proper funeral. When that's done, I'm getting my money and I'm gone."

That was all I needed to hear. I had to get word to someone. I thought of Francie first, but I knew what she'd say. She'd try to convince me to come home with her. She'd already told me several times that I could live in their guest room. And I appreciated the offer more than I could say, but it would mean staying indoors until Aunt Luanne came home.

I couldn't tell Francie about the men plotting to hijack another train, so I put a coded message in Roxy's Girl Scout book and asked Francie to give it to her. I said it was urgent. God alone knows why she took it and didn't ask questions.

And then I prayed. If Roxy could decipher the message, she'd know what to do.

Debbie felt a thrill of anticipation. She knew something most *Saundustee Secrets* readers wouldn't—what the message said. She read about Francie and James bringing the handbook to the Davises' house. Roxy had decoded the message and taken off on her bike the next day, June 15, without telling any of the Davises, including Caroline.

Roxy
Jade was hiding in the cave when I arrived. She was paler and thinner than the last time I'd seen her, and the haunted look in her eyes scared me. She wouldn't tell me what was

going on, just told me to follow her. We walked through the woods, the late afternoon sun casting strange shadows. I kept imagining they were men, hiding in the trees. Jade assured me the men had left, though she didn't think they'd gone far.

When we reached the railroad tracks, I felt as if I'd been punched in the stomach. I couldn't breathe, and my heart raced. Massive logs blocked the tracks. Minutes after leaving the station, the 5:22 freight train would hit the barricade and derail.

And there was nothing we could do about it. We were powerless. We couldn't lift even one of the huge logs. I started to cry. "I told the police the men were going to hijack the train like before. They'll be waiting at the station. The train will stop and then move on, and they'll think the call was a prank. We have to do something. Maybe set the logs on fire?" The logs were damp from a week of rain and would never light. But we had to try.

Jade didn't answer. She took off running through the woods. I thought she was getting matches. I started to search for dry kindling. I looked at my watch. 5:15. We didn't have time to start a fire. "Dear God, please. Make something go wrong with the engine. Or let them see the logs in time. Or something. Anything."

I heard Jade crashing through the underbrush, and then I saw her, bare legs streaked with blood. She jumped on top of the largest log.

"Jade, no! What if they can't stop?"

And then I saw what she'd gone back for. In her hand she held a compact. She opened it, and the mirror reflected the sunlight.

I stared in awe as she flashed out a message. I'd learned Morse code from the same handbook that had brought me here. D-A-N-G-E-R S-T-O-P D-A-N-G-E-R S-T-O-P D-A-N-G-E-R S-T-O-P

But no train came.

"They must be holding it at the station," I said.

"But they'll let it continue when they don't find anything."

We waited. Soon the sun would be too low. Jade continued to signal, catching the last rays of light.

And then we heard the rumble, saw the smoke. "Get out of the way!" I yelled, but Jade didn't move.

What if she didn't have the angle right? What if the engineer didn't see it? What if—

The squeal of metal on metal as the train hit its brakes was the sweetest sound I'd ever heard. Jade jumped down but continued to signal. The train whistle answered. C-F-M. "What does it mean?" I yelled over the din of screeching brakes.

Jade jumped off the tracks and pulled me toward the woods. "Confirmed." She was half laughing and half crying. "Let's get out of here."

We ran through the woods and up to the top of the bluff. We got there as the engine came to a halt about thirty feet from the blockage.

I threw my arms around Jade, and we both sobbed. "We saved the train," she said, laughter bubbling up again. "And the sugar."

And then we watched in shock as men poured out of every car. Hundreds of men, all in uniform.

Jade sank to the ground. My knees weakened at the same time, and I crumpled beside her.

It wasn't a freight train.

We'd saved a train full of soldiers.

CHAPTER TWENTY-THREE

Debbie pulled into the parking lot in front of Reese Hall at Camp Saundustee on Tuesday evening, but instead of getting out, she sat in silence for a moment, reflecting on the past three weeks.

Three weeks ago, she'd never met anyone who lived in Japan. Now she had invitations to visit Hoshi and Suki. Three weeks ago, she'd never heard of Roxy Britton or Jade Tanaka. Now, these women she wouldn't meet until she reached heaven were part of her life story.

Three weeks ago, she would have dreaded meeting Sara Loring. Today, she was eager for the opportunity to finally say the things her teenage self hadn't known how to express.

Tonight's Girl Scout meeting was part of what Carmen called "a reconnaissance mission to collect teasers." Before arriving in Dennison, she had contacted Camp Saundustee and spoken to Sara, who had referred her to Ashling. She'd also hired a local photographer. Tonight, with Girl Scouts, their families, camp staff, and members of the Chamber of Commerce present, they would take pictures to be used for promotions, give away some books, and stir up enthusiasm for the official book launch, which would take place right here a week after Roxy's memorial service.

With a deep exhale, Debbie tugged on the car door handle. But at that moment, her phone rang. Nathan Wade, her military contact. She smiled as she answered. She'd told him Jade's code about the 5:22 train. Had he learned anything she hadn't read in *Saundustee Secrets*? "Hi, Nate."

"Hey. I've only got a minute, but I had to call and tell you what I found out. Did you know the 5:22 was a troop train?"

As quickly and concisely as she could, she summed up what she'd learned from Roxy's book.

"Wow. Get me a copy of that book. Do you know what happened to the men who tried to derail the train?"

"No. I couldn't find anything."

"That's because the army kept it all on the down-low. Trying to minimize fear, I imagine. Anyway, they were found about a mile from where the train stopped. They were in a truck that had crashed into a tree. They confessed to everything. One of the guys was working at the depot when they stole the first load of sugar. He put sand in the engine oil so the train had to sit there overnight waiting for repairs. They tried to stop the next shipment from Great Lakes Sugar Company, but the schedule got changed so that the shipment came on a different train, while the soldiers came in on the one that was originally going to be sugar. The weirdest thing was that when the men were found, they both seemed to be having some kind of cardiac event."

She gasped. "Monkshood."

"What?"

"Minnie Franklin, one of the girls who was hiding Jade, overheard the men saying that before they left, they were going to put flowers on the grave of the man they killed. They must have thought the monkshood was pretty. They had no idea they were poisoning themselves with it."

"Whoa. They killed someone? From what I read, they were questioned about a body found in a shallow grave on the Saundustee property but were never convicted. I think you've solved an eighty-year-old cold case."

After saying goodbye to Nate, Debbie walked into Reese Hall carrying the white box marked GIRL SCOUTS WWII. Carmen, Talia, and Hoshi were already there. Greg and the boys helped them set up picture boards, while Ashling, Tiffany, and Janet set out trays of cookies and pitchers of lemonade.

This had been Roxy's wish, to start the book tour she would miss here in the place where the *Saundustee Secrets* story had played out. She had told Carmen she wanted the first books, signed by her a month before she died, to be given away to the next generation of Girl Scouts.

The door opened behind Debbie, and Suki walked in with Mrs. Porter. Mindy and her entourage trailed behind them, their expressions making it clear that they'd rather be anywhere else. Had Mrs. Porter forced them to come?

After greeting them, Debbie stood alone in the foyer, taking in the black-and-white photos that lined the walls and thinking of all she'd learned from Roxy and Jade. Theirs was more than a simple story. It was a profound lesson in forgiveness, grace, and humility.

As if called by the thoughts that caused her heart to race, a door opened and Sara stepped out of her office. "Debbie!" Her wide smile seemed so genuine.

As Sara strode across the foyer, Debbie set the box on a table and received her welcoming hug. "Hi, Sara. Can we talk?"

"Of course. Come into my office." She led the way into a small room with a cluttered desk in front of a bank of file cabinets. Instead of sitting behind the desk, she motioned to an alcove, unseen from the door, where two comfortable stuffed chairs sat facing each other.

They sat, and Debbie wiped her damp palms on her knees. "I owe you a very long-overdue apology."

Sara simply smiled.

Was it possible she had somehow forgotten? "That summer you were here, I kind of got lost, caught up in wanting to be popular over wanting to be a good person."

"Isn't that the story of every girl at fourteen?" Sara said with a smile.

"Maybe. But I hurt you because of it." She couldn't meet Sara's eyes. The shame from thirty years before felt fresh. "I should have at least tried to stop them. I could have—"

Sara laid a hand over Debbie's, silencing her. "I could tell how bad you felt. And I know you did everything in your power to make it up to me."

Debbie's mouth opened, but she couldn't form a response.

"Yes, I was hurt. One of the counselors had told me you and Janet were two girls I could trust. And then I couldn't. But it was so obvious when you realized you'd made a mistake and you felt terrible about it. Debbie, you and Janet were the reasons I didn't leave camp. Even though you didn't put it into words, you showed me what repentance looks like. You were the nicest girls here, and I was so grateful to be sharing a tent with you."

"But I heard your family moved because you were struggling."

"That's true, but camp was a small part of that. We moved to be closer to my grandparents, to a place where I could have a fresh start and a larger support system from my family. I went to speech therapy, stopped stuttering, and started making friends."

"Oh," Debbie said, her mind reeling.

Sara folded her hands and leaned in. "But here's the part you really need to hear. Because of you and Janet, I stayed in Girl Scouts. Because of that, I ended up in a position where I could fight to keep the camp open when the board wanted to close it. Now hundreds of girls attend every year. And on opening day of each camp, every girl hears the story of the girl who picked on me but repented, and the two girls who changed my life because they befriended and defended me when no one else would."

Debbie was still dabbing at her eyes when Talia and Hoshi began talking. Greg sat beside her, his arm resting on the back of her chair in support, though she hadn't had time to tell him the reason for her tears. Jade's and Roxy's granddaughters brought the story to life, even though, as they'd said in their introduction, they'd heard it barely a year before Jade died.

When they got to the part about finding the railroad tracks blocked and Jade signaling the train, a gasp broke the silence in the crowd.

Ashling, sitting to the side on the slightly raised platform, stood. "Mindy? Are you all right?"

Mindy stood, her hand over her mouth. "I…I know this story. I've heard it since I was a little girl. My great-grandfather called it the train angel story. He was the engineer on that train. He never knew who signaled him to stop. Jade saved my great-grandfather's life and all the other lives on that train." Her chin trembled with emotion. "If she hadn't, I wouldn't be here." Slowly, she scanned the faces in the room until she found the girl with long black hair who sat with her two blond friends instead of her host family.

"Suki, I am so sorry. I've been so wrong, so awful." As if suddenly realizing where she was and how many people were watching, she sank back onto her chair. "I'm going to make it right."

Suki's smile could have illuminated a cave at midnight.

Carmen, who'd been sitting next to Ashling, walked to the podium, Talia and Hoshi stepping aside to make room for her. Carmen's gaze was riveted on Mindy. "Honey, what you just did, that very brave thing? I can't think of anything that would honor Roxy and Jade more, or a more perfect way to end our talk. Thank you, from the bottom of my heart."

She invited all the girls to the book table for their free copy of *Saundustee Secrets* and a T-shirt. She held up one of the shirts. On it were Japanese characters Debbie now recognized, next to the numbers 5:44. Under it were the words LOVE YOUR ENEMIES, BLESS THEM THAT CURSE YOU.

Debbie was about to say something about Jade and Roxy's story coming full circle when Nomi approached them. Tears sparkled in her eyes, and her entire countenance was softer than Debbie had ever seen it. She held out a small white card. "I thought you should see this. Suki gave it to me."

On the card were several hand-drawn Japanese symbols and the words *Nomi. In Japanese, it means beautiful, pleasant, delightful.*

Nomi took a shaky breath and gave a wobbly smile. "I suppose that at long last, I should start living up to my name. I've been so caught up in my own old pain for so long that I didn't realize how much I was spreading it to those around me. I'd like to make a fresh start with breakfast at the café tomorrow and then give an honest review. I'll take the old ones down." With that, she walked away.

Still stunned, Debbie took in a sight that brought tears to her eyes. Minnie approached Carmen, Talia, and Hoshi, clutching a copy of *Saundustee Secrets* to her chest. "I still have one question the book didn't answer. Why did Roxy keep the monkshood flower?"

Carmen smiled. "The explanation was in her original manuscript, but she worried someone might try to do what she did, so we removed it. Roxy picked two flowers, with gloves on, of course. She sealed them in cellophane and gave one to Jade in a card with a quote from your grandfather. 'Beauty and evil often live side by side. Walk—"

"'Walk in wisdom and focus on the beauty.'" Minnie swiped at a tear with trembling fingers. "Those words have carried our family through so much."

An hour later, more tired yet more content than she'd felt in a long time, Debbie walked out of the hall with Greg. Unlike when she'd walked in, her arms were empty. With Kim's texted blessing, she'd loaned the Girl Scout book to Carmen for Diana's enjoyment, along with everything she'd found in it. Carmen had thanked her on Diana's behalf and promised that it would be returned for display in the place where the story had begun.

Greg put his arm around her as they walked to her car. After a few feet, he stopped. "Make a wish, Debbie."

Overhead, a bright swath of light flashed across the inky black sky dotted with stars. She leaned into him. "No need. All my wishes have already come true."

Dear Reader,

I hope you were inspired by Roxy's and Jade's resourcefulness and bravery. As soon as I received the green light from our wonderful editors, I ordered a 1941 Girl Scout handbook. Holding that thick book in my hands made the story come to life. It reminded me of an army field manual more than a guide to prepare teens for life.

I currently have two teenage granddaughters. As I wrote, I tried to imagine them dealing with the challenges Jade and Roxy faced. Would they have the tools and the emotional fortitude? It has me pondering what things my grandchildren need to learn in the next few years before they leave home. If nothing else, I hope I can be an example of living out Matthew 5:44.

Have Debbie, Janet, Roxy, Jade, and friends given you some things to ponder too? Being able to challenge and encourage while entertaining are some of the things I enjoy most about writing fiction. I love working with characters who deal with the same weaknesses and struggles I'm trying to overcome. Sometimes I learn a thing or two from them!

Most of us will never be falsely suspected of espionage or unjustly incarcerated, but most of us have experienced being gossiped about, laughed at, criticized, or even bullied.

The way we respond to those things says a lot about the condition of our hearts. In our humanity, we may be tempted to react with anger, resentment, or lashing out, but like any habit, forgiveness and repentance can be learned. Repetition is the key. We fail, we apologize or offer grace, we ask God to help us be better next time, and we start over. Think of it as a cardio workout for the soul.

Thanks for spending time with the Whistle Stop Café crowd. Wish we could sit down together and enjoy a peppermint mocha and a couple of Salvation Army doughnuts as we remind each other to "Love your enemies and pray for those who persecute you." We can do this!

Blessings,
Becky

ABOUT the AUTHOR

ecky Melby writes contemporary women's fiction, time slip novels, and cozy mysteries. She is a weekly blogger on Facebook at *Fill My Cup, Lord*. Becky and her husband, Bill, call Wisconsin home. They are the parents of four sons and have fifteen grandchildren. When not writing or spoiling grandchildren, Becky may be found feeding chickens, riding on the back of their Honda Gold Wing motorcycle, or touring the country in their RV.

A GLIMPSE of the PAST

Their Lives Would Never Be the Same

Imagine being a sixteen-year-old girl living in Los Angeles in December of 1941. It's almost Christmas. Your days are filled with school and friends. The biggest concerns on your mind revolve around what to wear, who to invite to your slumber party, what to buy your best friend for Christmas, and wondering if that boy sitting behind you in history is going to ask you to the Friday night dance.

And then, in a single day, everything changes. The country where your parents were born, where your grandparents still live, has attacked the United States. Suddenly, store owners, teachers, police officers—people you once trusted—are keeping their distance, looking at you as if you are the enemy. Even though you and your parents are American citizens.

Less than three months later, you're huddled around the radio in your living room with your parents, aunts, uncles, cousins, and neighbors. All you know is that an important announcement is coming. And then the radio crackles and the newscaster's words shatter another piece of your already confusing world. President Franklin D. Roosevelt has issued Executive Order 9066, authorizing the forced removal of all persons "deemed a threat to national security" from the West Coast to "relocation centers" further inland. The adults in the room begin talking over each other. You're trying to make sense of their words. And then someone says, "That means us."

Imagine being the parents of a sixteen-year-old girl, sitting in that room as the consequences of the executive order begin to sink in. What will this do to her? What does it mean for her future? Will you be separated? What is a relocation center?

Imagine being a pastor whose life's work is translating the writings of pillars of the church into the language of your homeland. All of that is about to come to a halt. For how long? What will happen to the manuscripts in your desk drawer, the ones you've worked on for months?

Over the next six months, more than 120,000 men, women, and children were moved to barbed-wire-surrounded guarded relocation centers in California, Colorado, Utah, Arizona, and Arkansas. Nearly 70,000 of the evacuees were American citizens. The government made no charges against them, but there were no avenues for them to appeal their incarceration. The only furnishings in the camp barracks were cots and coal stoves. Residents shared common bathrooms and laundry facilities. Hot water was a luxury that wasn't always available.

Some churches and individuals protested and offered assistance. They lobbied the government, provided storage for evacuees' possessions, and sent supplies to camps. In May of 1942 the National Japanese American Student Relocation Council (NJASRC) was formed to help young adult detention camp residents attend colleges in the Midwest and the East Coast. Thanks to their efforts, more than 4,000 students were able to attend more than 600 institutions.

Some citizens, like Roxy's mother, became sponsors, providing employment and places to live, often in the Midwest, for Japanese Americans who completed an FBI background check to prove their loyalty to the United States. After the war, many churches helped former detainees find jobs and reclaim their property. The thought brings some measure of comfort to an ugly piece of our country's history, though it doesn't excuse it.

FROM the HOME-FRONT KITCHEN

1917 Homemade Girl Scout Cookie Recipe

(Makes six to seven dozen cookies)

Ingredients:

1 cup butter

1 cup granulated sugar (plus additional for sprinkling on top)

2 eggs, beaten

2 tablespoons milk

1 teaspoon vanilla

2 cups flour

1 teaspoon salt

2 teaspoons baking powder

Directions:

1. Cream butter and sugar.
2. Add eggs, then milk, vanilla, flour, salt, and baking powder.
3. Refrigerate for at least 1 hour.
4. Preheat oven to 375°F.
5. Roll dough ½ inch thick.
6. Cut into trefoil shapes or circles.
7. Sprinkle with sugar.
8. Bake 8 to 10 minutes or until the edges begin to brown.

Read on for a sneak peek of another exciting book in the Whistle Stop Café Mysteries *series!*

RUMORS ARE FLYING

BY JEANETTE HANSCOME

Janet Shaw tied a brand-new red-and-white checked apron over her I'M A WHISK-TAKER T-shirt. She checked the bakery case to make sure she hadn't neglected any of the Whistle Stop Café's most popular offerings, though she'd added some fun fall goodies to lure people in on this first Monday after Labor Day. With school in full swing and the tourist season officially over, it felt like the perfect time to introduce flavors like pumpkin and cranberry. Today, the featured treat was decadent pumpkin mini muffins with chocolate chips.

Her best friend and business partner, Debbie Albright, finished writing the breakfast and lunch specials on the chalkboard behind the counter then inhaled deeply. "Those muffins smell like heaven."

Janet admired the bakery tray she'd slid into the case, with its neat rows of puffy pumpkin goodness speckled with semisweet chocolate. "They really do, if I do say so myself." *The first time I heard about pumpkin baked goods with chocolate chips, I thought* it sounded strange. But now it's one of my favorite combinations. The flavors complement each other so well."

Debbie drew a little flourish under her list of specials.

BREAKFAST: DENVER OMELET WITH HOME FRIES OR FRUIT
LUNCH: BLT WITH AVOCADO AND CHOICE OF FRIES,
SIDE SALAD, OR SOUP
SOUP OF THE DAY: HEARTY VEGETABLE

Debbie opened her apron pocket and dropped the chalk into it. "There we go. My attempt at creative lettering isn't quite as impressive as those muffins of yours. But it'll do for now."

"To be completely honest, I'm trying these muffins out on the customers before facing a much more brutal audience tomorrow."

"That's right. You start your workshop at the middle school tomorrow, you brave soul."

"Oh, it won't be that bad," Janet said, though she wasn't sure if she was trying to convince her friend or herself. "If the kids get too rambunctious, Julian will protect me. Besides, the Culinary Arts Club teacher, Mrs. Sloan, will be there."

Julian Connor—the teenage son of Debbie's boyfriend, Greg—had been the one to recommend that Janet teach a workshop to kickstart the new school year for the Culinary Arts Club. As Miranda had explained to Janet, the club usually only met once a week, but for the special September workshop, Janet would teach on Tuesday, Wednesday, and Thursday for the first week, and pop in for the regular Thursday afternoon meeting the next week to see how the kids applied what they learned.

Debbie strolled to the café entrance and unlocked the door. "Maybe you'll discover a baking prodigy."

"Wouldn't that be cool?" She'd already been dreaming of the possibility. "Inspiring the next generation of bakers is an exciting prospect. Although, right now, I'll be happy to make it through next week without making anyone cry, having to break up a fight, or dealing with a roomful of eye rolls because my recipes are totally lame."

"I don't think kids say 'totally lame' anymore."

"Well, the equivalent of it then."

"You'll be great." Debbie flipped the Open sign.

Janet busied herself with early morning customers stopping in for lattes, pastries, or a quick breakfast before work. A half hour after the café opened, Harry Franklin walked in with his dog, Crosby, at his side like always. Behind them, a dark-haired young man pushed Ray Zink's wheelchair.

Harry held the door open. "Look who's joining me for breakfast this morning."

Ray pointed over his shoulder. "Jake here recently joined the staff at Good Shepherd and offered limo service this morning."

Debbie grabbed menus from the slot near the cash register. "Good morning, gentlemen. Nice to meet you, Jake." She escorted them to a table near the counter where they could chat with Debbie and Janet and any other locals who happened to stop in.

Janet went over to hug her friends. "Look at you Ray, out on the town like you're nineteen again."

Ray gave Janet a smile that revealed a bit of the nineteen-year-old that still lived inside the ninety-eight-year-old veteran. "When Harry invited me to breakfast, I couldn't resist."

Janet leaned down to pet Crosby. "Good to see you too, boy."

Jake parked Ray's wheelchair at the table. "Enjoy your breakfast, Ray. Call when you're ready to be picked up. No rush."

"Will do. Thanks, Jake."

Jake gave Crosby a pat on the head before heading out. The dog curled up at Harry's feet.

"Or maybe, after some of Janet's delicious, nutritious food, Ray will be cured and can drive himself home," Harry said.

Ray pumped his fists in the air. "Janet's miracle breakfast."

"You guys are too much." Janet started making her way to the bakery case to find something to send home with Ray and Harry as a treat for later.

Debbie set a menu and a coffee mug in front of each of them just as Greg Connor came in. Her whole face lit up. "Well, good morning, stranger."

Greg greeted her with a hug and a peck on the cheek. "Good morning, beautiful. Hello, Janet."

"Hello, there, Greg." Harry patted the empty chair beside his. "Want to join me and Ray for breakfast?"

"Thanks for the offer, Harry, but I better get my coffee and run. I'm meeting with the inspector on a house-flipping project I've finished in Uhrichsville. Can I take a raincheck, though?"

"Of course, you can."

While setting aside half a dozen mini pumpkin-chocolate chip muffins for Ray and Harry, Janet noticed the smile that had spread across Debbie's face and stuck after Greg called her beautiful. It was so nice to see Debbie finally giving in to her feelings for the handsome, good-hearted single dad. Janet had realized a long time ago that they were made for each other.

Janet took a large to-go cup off the stack for Greg. "What kind of coffee can I make for you, Greg?"

"Just a drip coffee with cream, and I think I'll take three of those pumpkin muffins with the chocolate chips as well. They smell amazing."

"Good choice."

Debbie took Harry's and Ray's breakfast orders and set the slip on the counter for Janet. "They made it easy for you. Two orders of pancakes with bacon and eggs over medium." Her eyes quickly shifted back to Greg. "How was the chamber of commerce meeting the other night? As fun-filled as always?"

Janet chuckled. A chamber of commerce meeting sounded about as fun-filled as a root canal. But it was one of Greg's passions, and with him excited about serving Dennison in that way, the group got a lot accomplished.

Greg took out his wallet. "Actually, it wasn't as boring as you might think. Christine Murphy, from the Dennison Preservation Society, was there to propose a plan to buy that old Victorian home where Vera's Nursery used to be."

Janet filled Greg's cup with coffee. "I miss Vera's Nursery. Back when it was open, she had the best section of flowers and plants in Dennison and Uhrichsville combined."

Since Vera retired and closed the store years ago, the 120-year-old house had fallen into disrepair. Over the summer, Janet had read the sad news that Vera passed away.

She was glad to hear that the preservation society wanted to put the old house to good use. Memories of the house filled her mind like the scent of coffee filled the café. According to the stories she heard from her mother, the house had belonged to the Townsend family until 1945, when Jonas Townsend was reported killed in action.

When Janet was growing up, the house had been the Center Stage Academy of Voice and Dance. Janet had often sneaked into the backyard with her dolls and pretended she lived there. She'd watched dance classes through the windows, taught by the fairylike Miss Olivia with her perfect posture and graceful movements. She'd heard voice lessons given by Randolf Carson, opera singer by night, voice teacher by day.

In Janet's mother's day, it had housed a small private school that outgrew the building and made way for an art studio. But the Townsend house was most famous for its history as a boardinghouse for soldiers returning from World War II, who either didn't have family or needed a place to recuperate from their time overseas and figure out their next step.

Janet handed Greg his cup of coffee and set the bag of muffins on the counter in front of him.

Debbie popped an extra muffin into the bag. "So, Vera's son and daughter-in-law didn't inherit the place after she passed?"

"Vera didn't actually own it. She rented it from the Grayson family, who bought it after Joe Townsend was killed. Chad Grayson and his wife, Theresa, just inherited it from Chad's father. But they think it's become a money pit and want to sell. I can't blame them. His dad could never afford to keep up with repairs after it was left to him, and the place has been renovated so many times it'll need a complete makeover. Other than a few plumbing updates and patching roof repairs, I don't think it's been updated since the 1970s. The Dennison Preservation Society wants to buy it and turn it into a museum."

Janet brought her attention back to Harry and Ray. She picked up the order slip. "I'll get right on this."

Ray stroked Crosby's head. "No rush."

Harry added a cream to his coffee. "We have all day to hang out here and make a nuisance of ourselves."

"Thanks, Harry. I really want to hear more about what the preservation society has planned." Janet put the order sheet in her pocket and relaxed against the back corner. "I'm curious why they want to turn it into a museum. We already have the depot museum right outside the café."

Greg took a couple of creamers out of one of the baskets on the counter. "This would be a lot different than the one here at the train station. They proposed an idea to create a place called the Dennison House. It will present the typical 1940s home, celebrate the house's years as a boardinghouse for soldiers returning from World War II, and be open for tours, field trips, and special events. Ladies' teas, that sort of thing."

"I think that sounds wonderful. So many of those old Victorians go up for sale, only to have the buyers gut them and update everything until they're no longer authentic and lose their historical charm."

"That's the exact point Christine brought up. The preservation society wants to restore the house to its former glory. There was even talk of making it part of the Christmas Train experience. They mentioned some fundraising events for the renovation that sound like a lot of fun."

Janet reached for the coffee carafe. If Harry and Ray were being so patient, the least she could do was offer them each a warm-up. "So the chamber of commerce approved the plan?"

"We approved the idea of creating the Dennison House, but the Dennison Preservation Society will have to put in a bid for the house like anyone else would. We explained to Christine that we didn't have the authority to tell the Graysons who to sell their house to. The house needs a thorough inspection, and I'm sure it will also need extensive repairs, including a new roof, so the society has time to consider a budget and maybe even apply for some grants."

Debbie pulled a couple of napkins out of the nearest dispenser and put them in Greg's bag. "I bet the Graysons will like the idea of selling to a group like the Dennison Preservation Society. It'll give the house a purpose. They'll get to see it make a difference in the community."

"I sure hope so. As one who is constantly buying and selling houses, I know it might be tricky selling to a community group that's basically a nonprofit. But if they get as excited about the idea of the Dennison House as everyone was last night, the preservation society should be a shoo-in when the time comes to sell."

Janet handed Greg his bag and coffee. "It would be sad to see someone outbid them when they already have a plan for the house."

Greg paid. "I don't see this turning into a huge bidding war. The house has been through so many transformations that it'll need quite a bit of work. Personally, I think a museum is the perfect use for the place."

Janet took Ray and Harry's order out of her pocket. "So it's okay to start getting excited about the idea of a new tourist draw?"

"Cautiously excited, sure." Greg held up his cup as if in a toast. "I better be off." He gave Debbie a hug and a peck on the cheek that made her blush. "See you later."

She smiled. "See ya." After Greg left, Debbie faced Janet. "Well, that's exciting news."

"It is very exciting. Almost as exciting as me finally getting Harry's and Ray's breakfast started. It'll be right out, guys." Janet made her way to the kitchen.

She cracked four eggs onto the griddle and made the pancakes extra-large, musing all the while. A 1940s-style house would be a great draw. And if the Dennison Preservation Society did find a way to add it to the Christmas Train experience, it could breathe new life into a beloved tradition.

When Janet brought out the order, the pace in the café had started to pick up. She offered some fresh blueberries to her friends as an extra topping. "So, what do you two think of Greg's news about the Townsend house?"

Ray drizzled syrup over his pancakes. "I think it's a fine idea. Jonas would be pleased to have his home turned into a museum."

"Ray and Jonas were good friends," Harry told Janet.

Ray popped a bite of egg into his mouth. "Yep, we were friends from the time we sat next to each other in the first grade. We had our first trip to the corner together for clowning around during spelling. Twelve years later, we enlisted in the Army a day apart. Sadly, he was one of the friends who didn't come home."

Janet wished for time to freeze so she could join Ray at the table for a while and hear about his old friend Jonas. Until that moment, Jonas's name had been one more detail of the history of an old house. Now, he was Ray Zink's childhood friend. "I'm sorry you lost such a good friend, Ray."

"I haven't thought about him in a long time. The whole story behind how the Townsend house went up for sale was tragic." Ray set his fork down. "Before we both enlisted, Jonas was going out with a sweet girl named Gracie Pike. Everyone knew they would marry one day. A few months after he left for basic training, Jonas's parents were both killed in an accident. Then Jonas was killed in war. The couple who bought it opened it to soldiers who needed a place to stay a year later. But to me, it never stopped being Jonas's house." Ray picked up his fork again, but instead of scooping up another bite, he let it hover while his eyes drifted to nothing in particular.

Before Janet could ask if he was okay, a group of women came in for breakfast, sending Janet back to the kitchen to whisk eggs into omelets, fry sausage, and line the griddle with rows of pancakes. Her excitement over the idea of adding a place like the Dennison House to her hometown's historic offerings got edged out by the distant look she'd seen in Ray's eyes. This wasn't the first time she'd heard him talk about friends who had died in the war, but she sensed something different when Ray shared about Jonas. What was it?

Seeing Jonas's house put to use might be good for Ray. Janet edged her spatula under a golden pancake and flipped it neatly. She pictured Ray and Harry being some of the first to tour the Dennison

House. They could offer suggestions for how to make the house authentic according to their own memories, especially with seasonal decorations.

She stacked three perfectly round pancakes on a plate. Maybe she could talk to the preservation society about dedicating the Dennison House to Jonas Townsend for his sacrifice. That would mean a lot to Ray.

As the breakfast rush tapered off, Janet took advantage of the slower pace to leave the heat of the kitchen and catch up with whichever locals happened to be lingering in the café. She found Ray and Harry still at their table while Crosby tracked Debbie's every move from his spot beside Harry's chair. He was rewarded when she dropped a bit of toast on the floor in front of him.

"You spoil him, Debbie," Harry told her, but there was no censure in his tone.

"No, I teach him to expect the same treatment here that I know he gets at home," Debbie replied with a grin. "I'm still thinking about the Townsend house. I've seen pictures of the place from the forties. If the preservation society can make the Dennison House happen, and Christine is in charge, she'll turn it into something incredible. Especially at Christmas."

Janet went over to Harry and Ray's table and pulled out one of their extra chairs. "She could design it to be like Santa's Workshop." She put one hand on Ray's shoulder and the other on Harry's. "We have two elves right here."

Harry smacked the table. "I'm in."

The melancholy look that Janet saw in Ray's eyes when talking about Jonas was nowhere in sight now. "They can turn my wheelchair into Santa's sleigh."

Debbie set a stack of dishes in the bin behind the counter. "Too bad it isn't in a spot where passengers could see the house from the train windows. But still, they can see it on the way to the station."

"I know it's a bit premature to start making plans for the place," Janet admitted. "It's not a done deal yet. But I'm too excited. If it works out, it's going to be incredible."

"It is," Debbie agreed. She nodded toward the café entrance. "Do you want to finish cleaning this table, or do you want to take their order?"

A middle-aged couple stood patiently beside the counter.

Janet got her head back into the game of serving customers. "Welcome. Will this be for here or to go?"

"We'd like to eat here," the man replied.

"Glad to hear it. Feel free to have a seat anywhere you like, and we'll be right with you," Janet assured them.

The tall, ponytailed woman thanked Janet as the couple made their way to a table against the wall lined with framed World War II prints.

Debbie went over with two menus. Janet went behind the counter in case they wanted something sweet. "Are you new to Dennison or just visiting?"

"Visiting." The man took a menu.

The woman took the other and laid it in front of her on the table. "We're staying in one of the Pullmans for a few nights."

Janet took two glasses out of the rack behind her and filled them with water. "You're smart to take a vacation after school starts. The Pullmans were booked all summer long." She carried the water to them. "Where are you from?"

The woman drew her glass closer. "Lakewood. Our youngest daughter just went off to college at Case Western Reserve, so we're officially empty nesters now."

Janet savored the moment of familiarity. "My daughter is in her second year at Case Western. It's a great school. If you give me your daughter's name before you leave, I'll pass it on to Tiffany in case they cross paths."

The man nudged his wife. "See, Chloe will be fine."

The woman's eye grew a little teary. "She will. I know." She blinked hard and took a deep breath. "Thank you."

"My name's Janet." She gestured to her co-owner. "And that's Debbie. If you're staying in a Pullman, you'll probably be here often. We might as well know one another's names."

Harry waved across the café. "I'm Harry Franklin, and this is Crosby. You'll definitely see us again."

Ray raised his hand. "Ray Zink. Why don't you join us?"

"That sounds lovely. I'm Laney Farrell." Laney went over and shook Harry's hand and Ray's then took one of the free chairs at the table.

Her husband followed. "And I'm Brian."

Debbie set out fresh utensils for them. "What inspired you to choose Dennison for your first big trip as empty nesters? Not to put down our fine town or anything. I mean, we do have plenty of historic sites, and now is a great time to see them without having to fight the crowds. Our tourist season is about over."

Laney set her oversized tote bag on the floor. "Actually, we have a really big trip planned for October."

"Italy," Brian added.

"Good choice," Debbie said. "If I ever have a honeymoon, I want to go to Italy."

Janet made a mental note to pass that on to Greg. *I have a feeling that honeymoon is in your future.*

Laney picked up her menu. "This trip is more about checking out a house we're hoping to purchase for a B and B."

The idea of having a new bed-and-breakfast in Dennison as well as the preservation society's museum sent a fresh wave of excitement through Janet. She pictured summer tourists keeping both hopping from Memorial Day to Labor Day.

Debbie cleared an empty plate from the table behind Laney. "Would you like some coffee or tea while you look over the menu?"

Laney pulled a blue spiral notebook out of her tote bag. "Coffee sounds great."

Brian opened his menu. "Make that two, please."

Debbie headed toward the counter. "I'll make a fresh pot."

Janet noticed an empty basket of creamers and took it to the kitchen to replenish the selection. When she returned, the couple had moved their menus to the edge of the table to make room for the spiral notebook. Laney turned to a page that had a photo of an old house paper-clipped to the top.

"Are you ready to order?" Janet scooped up the menus and placed the basket in their place.

"I know it's not quite lunchtime, but a BLT sounds good," Laney said.

Debbie came over with the coffeepot and two mugs. "I consider a BLT the best of breakfast and lunch combined. Bacon and toast are breakfast foods, while the veggies are lunch foods." She took an order pad and pen out of her apron pocket.

Janet's gaze snagged on the picture in Laney's notebook. The house looked familiar.

Brian ordered a ham-and-egg scramble. Debbie jotted it down, tore off the order page, and handed it to Janet.

Laney moved the notebook aside and reached for the creamer basket. Janet sneaked another glance at the picture, now enhanced by midmorning sun. She froze at the sight of a large oak tree in front of the house, and a white painted gate leading to the backyard that was almost as familiar as the one where she'd grown up.

She folded Laney and Brian's order slip in half to keep her hands busy, so she wouldn't reach for the notebook and ask why they had a picture of the old Townsend house.

While you are waiting for the next fascinating story
in the Whistle Stop Café Mysteries, check out
some other Guideposts mystery series!

SAVANNAH SECRETS

Welcome to Savannah, Georgia, a picture-perfect Southern city known for its manicured parks, moss-covered oaks, and antebellum architecture. Walk down one of the cobblestone streets, and you'll come upon Magnolia Investigations. It is here where two friends have joined forces to unravel some of Savannah's deepest secrets. Tag along as clues are exposed, red herrings discarded, and thrilling surprises revealed. Find inspiration in the special bond between Meredith Bellefontaine and Julia Foley. Cheer the friends on as they listen to their hearts and rely on their faith to solve each new case that comes their way.

The Hidden Gate
A Fallen Petal
Double Trouble
Whispering Bells
Where Time Stood Still
The Weight of Years
Willful Transgressions

MYSTERIES of MARTHA'S VINEYARD

Priscilla Latham Grant has inherited a lighthouse! So with not much more than a strong will and a sore heart, the recent widow says goodbye to her lifelong Kansas home and heads to the quaint and historic island of Martha's Vineyard, Massachusetts. There, she comes face-to-face with adventures, which include her trusty canine friend, Jake, three delightful cousins she didn't know she had, and Gerald O'Bannon, a handsome Coast Guard captain—plus head-scratching mysteries that crop up with surprising regularity.

A Light in the Darkness
Like a Fish Out of Water
Adrift
Maiden of the Mist
Making Waves
Don't Rock the Boat
A Port in the Storm
Thicker Than Water
Swept Away
Bridge Over Troubled Waters
Smoke on the Water
Shifting Sands
Shark Bait
Seascape in Shadows

Storm Tide
Water Flows Uphill
Catch of the Day
Beyond the Sea
Wider Than an Ocean
Sheeps Passing in the Night
Sail Away Home
Waves of Doubt
Lifeline
Flotsam & Jetsam
Just Over the Horizon

A NOTE FROM the EDITORS

We hope you enjoyed another exciting volume in the Whistle Stop Café Mysteries series, published by Guideposts. For over seventy-five years, Guideposts, a nonprofit organization, has been driven by a vision of a world filled with hope. We aspire to be the voice of a trusted friend, a friend who makes you feel more hopeful and connected.

By making a purchase from Guideposts, you join our community in touching millions of lives, inspiring them to believe that all things are possible through faith, hope, and prayer. Your continued support allows us to provide uplifting resources to those in need. Whether through our communities, websites, apps, or publications, we inspire our audiences, bring them together, and comfort, uplift, entertain, and guide them. Visit us at guideposts.org to learn more.

We would love to hear from you. Write us at Guideposts, P.O. Box 5815, Harlan, Iowa 51593 or call us at (800) 932-2145. Did you love *When You Wish Upon a Star*? Leave a review for this product on guideposts.org/shop. Your feedback helps others in our community find relevant products.

Find inspiration, find faith, find Guideposts.

Shop our best sellers and favorites at
guideposts.org/shop

Or scan the QR code to go directly to our Shop

Find more inspiring stories in these best-loved Guideposts fiction series!

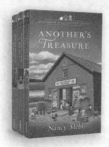

Mysteries of Lancaster County

Follow the Classen sisters as they unravel clues and uncover hidden secrets in Mysteries of Lancaster County. As you get to know these women and their friends, you'll see how God brings each of them together for a fresh start in life.

Secrets of Wayfarers Inn

Retired schoolteachers find themselves owners of an old warehouse-turned-inn that is filled with hidden passages, buried secrets, and stunning surprises that will set them on a course to puzzling mysteries from the Underground Railroad.

Tearoom Mysteries Series

Mix one stately Victorian home, a charming lakeside town in Maine, and two adventurous cousins with a passion for tea and hospitality. Add a large scoop of intriguing mystery, and sprinkle generously with faith, family, and friends, and you have the recipe for *Tearoom Mysteries*.

Ordinary Women of the Bible

Richly imagined stories—based on facts from the Bible—have all the plot twists and suspense of a great mystery, while bringing you fascinating insights on what it was like to be a woman living in the ancient world.

To learn more about these books, visit Guideposts.org/Shop